the "rest & relationships" issue

"Sometimes it's important to work for that pot of gold. But other times it's essential to take time off and to make sure that your most important decision in the day simply consists of choosing which color to slide down on the rainbow."

>> Douglas Pagels

FEATURED TEACHERS & ARTISTS

Darcy Le Fleming

The Intricate and Meditative Beadwork of Snails + Fairydust

82

LaRissa Paras

Guiding Teen Girls Toward their Own Power, Value, & Courage

76

Maggie Cure

Insights on Family, Lesson Ideas, and Homeschooling from a Faith-Filled Teacher Mom

42

Brittany Jeltema

Classroom Renovation Decisions That Lead to Stronger Community & Build Relationships

30

Sara Langelier

Sewing a Custom Teacher Wardrobe from Scratch

24

Shannon Olsen

Reimagining Each Classroom of Students as a Family

98

never lose sight of the fact that the most important yardstick of your success will be how you treat other people - your family, friends, and coworkers, and even strangers you meet along the way.
>> barbara bush

 *if you get tired, learn to rest, not quit.* >> banksy

Inbox Hacks for Teacher Productivity	8
School Day Workout Plan	10
Bring Your Book Idea to Life	12
Unmasking Math Anxiety	18
Building Classroom Community	22
Communication with Parents ... Simplified!	50
The Widespread Impact of Sleep	52
Hands in the Earth: Plant Activities for Kids	56
Teacher to New Teacher: A Conversation with a Mentor	86
Immune Support Cocktail	87
Educator Burnout Stats, Trends, and Solutions	88
Boost Your Bath with Healthy Ingredients	92
5 Ways to Style a Jumpsuit	94
I've Got Your Back: The Class as a Family	98

IN EVERY ISSUE

From the Editor	4
Bell Work	7
Classroom Tour	70
Discover	68
Passing Notes	90
Mind of a Creator	82
Inspiration From...	104

18 Unmasking Math Anxiety

92 Boost Your Bath: Healthy Recipes

FROM THE EDITOR...

There are some careers that are more like a calling than a job. Nurses, law enforcement officers, armed service members, priests and ministers, and social workers, for example, often go into their chosen field to provide a service they are passionate about. They don't choose the job because it's easy. They don't choose it because it offers big profits. They don't even choose it to move up a career ladder and gain fame or success. They follow their hearts because they care about those they want to help.

Teaching is one of these jobs. We teach because we feel that it's important for good people to teach our youth and make a difference. The career almost becomes its own lifestyle. The effects of this can reach into all the different realms of a teacher's life, and impact many different relationships.

This issue centers around relationships. Most of the relationships we are looking at here are within the school, but we also need to remember those relationships that live outside the building, but are intertwined with teaching life. A strong commitment to teaching reaches into home life, every corner of the brain, and the deepest part of the soul. Anyone who loves a teacher eventually starts to understand and accept what "my kids" means, and starts to realize how many hours a teacher really clocks per week.

I believe that teacher spouses deserve extra credit. Although it may not be on the same level as military spouses, anyone who marries a teacher is destined for certain hurdles. One evening, I woke up after drifting off over a stack of 8th grade math warm-up quizzes that I had not gotten through, only to find them all graded and stacked neatly, already entered in the gradebook. My husband claimed that the "quiz fairy" had visited while I slept.

Similarly, I sometimes forget when chatting with friends that I am not supposed to say that "my parents" teach kindergarten, when in reality only my mom does. But it's hard to remember that when my retired dad is in there volunteering so frequently, and is constantly telling us adorable stories about each kindergartener as if it's another of his own grandchildren. It's almost as if it's a team effort that is central to their marriage. The passion behind each individual teaching journey spreads across a wide network and requires a lot of family support. Let's take a moment to address each loved one today and thank them for their patience and support.

Our other key focus in this issue is rest. Rest, for a teacher, can mean keeping the immune system functioning well enough for flu season with little ones all around. Or it can mean taking a restorative health-boosting bath. Sometimes it just means preventing burnout. For students, rest can sometimes even prevent an ADHD misdiagnosis, obesity, or depression. Grab a cup of tea and enter into this issue to learn more, get inspired, and refresh and restore yourself along the way.

Let Snowday be your guide to a productive, thoughtful, passionate life as an educator AND as a creative, vibrant human soul!

- Brigid

SPOTLIGHT THEMES IN THIS ISSUE: REST & RELATIONSHIPS

REST

Both in terms of sleep and restoration, we're investigating problems and solutions. We're sharing the concerning facts about how many of our children and teens are sleep deprived, and how this hidden root cause gets misdiagnosed as ADHD or depression, or even is the reason behind a lot of the rising obesity in the U.S. Then, we are turning the focus to your own rest and relaxation, with specific recipes for boosting your bath. These add-ins will help you convert your mental self-care time into a physical body benefit as well.

Boost Your Bath >> 92
Teacher Burnout >> 88
The Impact of Sleep >> 52
Immune Boosting Cocktail >> 87

RELATIONSHIPS

A teacher's life is filled with a wide variety of meaningful relationships. We're taking a closer look at the different types of relationships that impact your career and life, including teacher-to-student relationships, teacher-to-teacher relationships, student-to-student relationships, teacher-to-parent relationships, and even teacher-to-administrator relationships.

Each of these is a gear in the machine that makes an entire school run smoothly. How can you improve the climate within your classroom, within your building, and within your district?

We're looking at the ways that the classroom environment plays a role in relationship building with a famous classroom "flipper" (renovation expert). Even the family aspect of close relationships comes into play, as we take a peek at a homeschool family with a faith-based teacher mom who knows how to beautifully integrate learning with life. You'll enjoy the different perspectives and the wide variety of inspiration!

"I've Got Your Back" - The Class as a Family Unit >> 98
Insights from a Faith Filled Teacher >> 42
Easier Communication with Parents >> 50
Mentor Teacher / Student Teacher Brainstorm >> 86
Building a Classroom Community >> 22
Strengthening Relationships Through Renovation >> 30

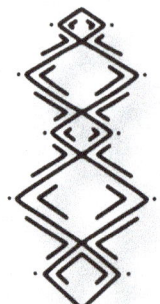

God's peace is joy resting.

His joy is peace dancing.

>> F.F. Bruce

Editor & Publisher
Brigid Danziger

Editing & Proofreading
Michael Dober

Writers
Kelly Barendt
Brigid Danziger
Carmen Myer
Elizabeth Ingram

Sponsored and Produced by
Math Giraffe, LLC

Follow On Instagram
@snowdaymagazine

Contact Us
editor@snowdaymagazine.com

Advertising
media@snowdaymagazine.com

Website
SNOWDAYMAGAZINE.COM

Copyright 2020

All rights reserved. Views, comments, and suggestions do not necessarily represent those of the publisher, and are provided as is. Snowday's editor and publisher disclaim any and all legal responsibility for the reader's use of any information included in this publication. Content given is not intended as a replacement for consulting an expert.

No portion of this publication may be reproduced without permission.

BELL WORK

"Jobs fill your pocket. Adventures fill your soul."

>> Jamie Lyn Beatty

Objective:
Travel smart by traveling light for your next professional development conference or vacation.

by LaRissa Paras
(featured on p. 76)

1. THINK "CAPSULE WARDROBE":
Choose a neutral color palette with color accents for accessories. Make sure all bottoms can be worn with multiple tops and vice versa.

2. GET THE DETAILS RIGHT:
Pack travel size toiletries and use clean contact lens cases for things like eye cream, gel, serum, etc. And don't forget that shopping at local pharmacies is a great way to replenish when you're abroad!

3. STRATEGIZE FOOTWEAR:
Wear your bulkiest shoes on the plane and pack your socks inside of your shoes in the suitcase.

4. PROTECT YOUR VALUABLES:
Choose a cross body purse with a thicker strap. Keep it hanging in front of you in crowded areas for safely storing your things. Also, keep cash in multiple locations, just in case.

5. SKIP THE LIBRARY:
Don't drag a ton of books with you. Go digital for a trip; books are super heavy. But, always have a small journal to record your thoughts and memories.

Some aspects of teaching can become really tedious. Don't let tackling your email inbox become one of them! Our email hacks are customized specifically for teachers to make your time spent on emails much more efficient and pleasant.

USE CANNED TEMPLATES

Do you find yourself typing out similar responses too often? It becomes tedious and time-consuming. It might be one of the reasons you tend to put emails on the back burner. You should try canned templates.

Canned templates are essentially generic email replies that can be sent to pretty much any recipient. They save you so much time, and also help you make better, quicker decisions because you're not working to compose a response.

So, invest a little time creating a collection of canned templates you will use often. This saves you time in the long run. Any good email service will allow you to set up canned templates, but because it's so popular, we'll share how to set up canned templates in Gmail.

How to Set Up Canned Templates in Gmail:
Step 1: Activate canned templates by going to Settings > Advanced > Templates
Step 2: Now, you can save emails you write as a canned template. When you're starting to type a response or a new email, click the three dots at the bottom (more options), and hover over Templates. Here, you can choose to save your template or choose an existing one.
Step 3: Start creating templates! Draft up some common responses, using our samples as a guide. You can do this for both your school inbox and your home email account.

Here are some example templates you might want to use to inspire you in writing your own!

sample canned responses

For when a parent emails you to inform you their child will be absent:
Hello there,
Thank you for letting me know! We will miss [Insert student's name], today. Please remind your child to complete the make-up work, which can be found [Insert classroom procedure].
Thank you!
[Your name]

For when a parent or student emails to ask you a question that can easily be found on the class page:
Hello,
Thank you for reaching out. I'm happy to help. The answer to this can be found on our class page [insert link to class page.] We've set it up so it can (hopefully) be easy for you to navigate. Please reach out with any further questions .
Best,
[Your name]

For when a student emails you asking for extra credit:
Hello,
Thank you for your concern about your grades in my class. As per our class syllabus, [Insert class policy]
See you in class,
[Your name]

For when a parent emails you about bringing in lunch for their child:
Hello,
I am sure [Insert student's name] will love that! Our lunch is from [insert times], and the school requires you to check in at the office.
Have a great day,
[Your name]

For when a student emails you late at night, asking for an extension for an assignment due at midnight:
Hello,
Thank you for your concern. However, you know I do not check my email after 8 pm. Our class syllabus states [Insert class policy]. I'd be glad to discuss partial credit at our next class.
Take care,
[Your Name]

For when you can't get to an email right away:
Hello there,
Thanks so much for getting in touch. I just wanted to let you know that I'm looking into it and will get back to you before [end of day/end of week] with an answer. If this is urgent, let me know and I'll try to get back to you sooner.
All the best,
[Your Name]

For when a parent sends you a nasty email:
Hello,
I am sorry to hear this, but want you to know I appreciate your investment in your child's education. [Either address the problem here or request a meeting on the phone or in person.]
Sincerely,
[Your Name]

For when you are reminding a parent or student an assignment is overdue:
Hello there,
This is a short reminder that I'm still waiting on [insert assignment]. Please get it back to me as soon as possible.
Best,
[Your Name]

inbox HACKS
to boost productivity

Reminders for canned templates:
A great canned template strategy doesn't mean an email can fit any single recipient in your address book without tweaking it. Canned responses need to be customizable. They should just give you a great head start.

Communication, especially with parents and students, should be warm and personal. You want them to know you truly care. This is why customizing your canned templates is so important. If you use canned templates without adding personal touches, your messages can come across as cold, dry, or just impersonal.

Remember, canned templates should not do the work for you. They should just be a good starting point, so you can be more efficient with the sentences and phrases you type frequently.

ENABLE "UNDO SEND"
We've all been there. You press send and then instantly regret it. Maybe you were hastily responding to a disgruntled parent. Maybe you just made a simple typo or forgot important information that may cause confusion. Whatever the predicament, there is an awesome, simple solution. Go to your email settings and enable "Undo Send." In Gmail, there's a drop down menu to choose the send cancellation period. 10 seconds should work.

RECEIVE FEWER EMAILS
(BY SENDING CLEARER EMAILS)
This hack may sound unimportant, but actually has a lot of power behind it. When composing an email, put yourself in the recipient's shoes. What possible questions could come up? Be proactive. If you are reminding a student about a late assignment, be sure to include extra details like where and when they should turn it in. By predicting upcoming questions, you're eliminating extra back and forth.

CUSTOMIZE YOUR SIGNATURE
You probably already have an email signature, but if not, save yourself from typing a goodbye signoff with your name at the end every single time you end an email message. Just go to your email settings and add a new signature. Instead of only inserting your name, customize it with your name, job title, and even a link to the class page. This will decrease the amount of replies and questions you get back! This leads into our next hack...

CREATE AN FAQ PAGE
If you find yourself being asked the exact same questions over and over, and subsequently typing out the exact same replies over and over, it's time you think about an FAQ page. Gather your most frequently asked questions, write a clear, succinct answer for each, and post on the class page. Next time parents or students come to you with identical questions, just direct them to the FAQ page.

Keep in mind that your FAQ page should be a living and up-to-date document. You should be adding questions and answers and editing past ones regularly, so your page is always relevant and informative.

SET LIMITS
Only check your email at certain times. Experts suggest scheduling out checking your email only 2-3 times a day. This helps you concentrate on the emails in your inbox at the moment, and it puts your mind at ease knowing that you will get to your inbox at some point. They also recommend you don't check your email first thing in the morning or at night.

TACKLE EACH EMAIL JUST ONCE
Only touch an email once, whenever possible. Your rule of thumb should be: If an email will take two minutes or less, do it right then and there. This minimizes clutter in your inbox and immediately crosses quick and easy tasks off your to-do list. Simple email replies will no longer take up headspace, and you'll also minimize the amount of clicking, which surprisingly does add up. Save yourself time by being disciplined.

recipe for a sneaking a FIT Teacher Workout
into each school day

As a teacher, you know time is of the essence! Often, we don't have (or make) the time to take care of our bodies, even though we all know the benefits, like improved heart health, stress relief, healthy joints, and so much more. Teaching is time-consuming and mentally and physically draining, so we don't always have the time or energy for a proper workout. Here are some easy exercises you can sprinkle in throughout a normal school day. Each small exercise is manageable, but together it all builds up over time!

Copy Machine Squats
Waiting for the copier to spit out your copies doesn't need to be tedious or time-consuming. Use this time to do squats. Stand with your feet a little wider than shoulder-width, and keep your arms parallel to the ground. Bend your knees and dip your body as low as you can go. Stand up quickly and repeat 20-30 times. This will get your heart rate up and it strengthens some of your body's biggest muscles!

Lunchtime Laps
While you're on lunch duty, try multi-tasking and walk laps around the lunchroom. You can easily do this while still keeping a close eye on students. (Sorry to all the early elementary teachers who will probably be too busy opening and helping students with lunches- this might not work for you!)

Recess Duty Hamstring Heel Taps
While standing around monitoring the kids during recess, bus duty, or other "supervisory duties," kick one heel back towards your butt. Lower it, and then kick the other leg. Repeat this 10 times to strengthen and stretch your hamstrings.

Coffee Brewing Calf Raises
While waiting for your coffee to brew (or monitoring a test), lightly hold the countertop or podium and step up on your toes, raising your calves. Step up and lower down repeatedly until you feel the burn!

Grading Leg Planks
While grading papers, sit on the edge of your chair with your feet on the floor, and knees at a 90-degree angle. Kick your right leg out straight and hold for 10-15 seconds. Switch legs and repeat 10-15 times.

After-school Wall Sits
Since no one needs their students seeing this, wait until everyone leaves and you have some privacy. Find a wall with some empty space to back up to. Stand with your feet hip-width apart and lower your rear end down until your knees make a 90 degree angle. Hold your arms out parallel to your thighs. Keep your back flat against the wall and hold the position for 30-60 seconds. Repeat if you can.

Before-School Tree Pose (or Any Yoga Pose)
Before school begins and the chaos of the day ensues, take 1-2 minutes (or more if you have them!) for yourself and do a yoga pose to focus on your breathing. Set an intention for the day. We recommend tree pose to help you feel strong and balanced. Stand and shift your weight to your right foot. Bring your left foot up so the sole is resting on your inner right thigh.

Subtle Storytime Ab Crunches
During storytime or any time you're sitting, clench your abdominals for a few seconds, then release and repeat until you start to feel the burn. Try doing it with each page turn, or get more ambitious and do one after each sentence. Think about bringing in your belly button to your spine. The motion in the abdomen should feel like it does when you say the word "hut" with emphasis.

Teaching Team Fitbit Challenges
If you all have fitbits, go on the app and choose a challenge. Each has different rules, duration, and number of players. Invite your teammates and go! Fitbits make challenges more straightforward, but you can still make up your own challenges too, using the Health App on your iPhone or a simple pedometer.

Calling Home Stretches
There are a ton of quick back, neck, and shoulder stretches that promote healthier joints and relieve stress. Next time you're on the phone with a parent, take the time to roll your shoulders back repeatedly. Sit facing straight on your chair, then place your right hand on the back of your chair then gently twist to face the wall behind you. Repeat on the other side.

Add Your Own!
Get creative with what you have available. Some of those "flexible seating" options can double as great step ups for a leg workout, balls for ab crunches, or cushions for sneaking in a quick floor workout. Sneak some 5 pound weights into your teacher cabinet. You can pull them out to use with one hand as you wipe down desks with the other, then... switch!

*Consult your physician before trying new exercises, or if you've had a past injury, and stop if anything causes pain.

Bring Your BOOK IDEA to Life

How to Make the Novel, Children's Book, or School Yearbook Inside your Mind Become a Printed Reality

by Kelly Barendt

There's just something about holding your fresh, new book in your hands, and flipping through the pages. As the author, it fills you with a sense of pride. You think, "I did that!" Any teacher can tell you that when someone knows the end product will be a published book, the quality and effort go through the roof.

There are multiple reasons that many teachers want to publish a book. Maybe you're having your students create a published book on a unit. Maybe, after seeing thousands of children's books or teen novels throughout your career, you have your own best-selling idea for a book. Maybe, you want a personal photo book, or you're in charge of publishing a school yearbook.

Whatever your reason, it's exciting to realize that now, self-publishing a book is easier than it ever has been, and doesn't have to cost a fortune!

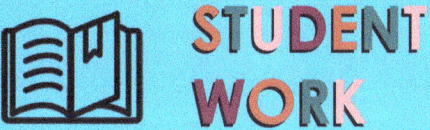

STUDENT WORK

If you plan to have students create and publish a book for a unit, imagine telling them they are going to be published authors! Here are some options you may want to check out.

Printi
This site offers a variety of books and booklets to choose from if you're thinking of publishing a class book! It offers high quality for a low-budget price. You upload PDF documents that meet their size requirements, and you're good to go!

Local Bookstore/ Printing Service
Contact your local bookstore or Printing Service (Office Max, etc.) to see if they would do some printing and binding for you. Be sure to mention the books were written by your students and they may offer a discount.

Studentreasures Publishing
Studentreasures Publishing allows your classroom to publish a book for free. First, choose the best classbook kit for your students. Then, you can have your class go through the steps for writing a book. Finally, get it published and receive a free deluxe hardcover copy of the collaborative book. They just ask that you send home order forms to parents to see if they would like a copy! 100% satisfaction is guaranteed.

School Mate Publishing
This company is similar to the one above. Each student submits two pages of writing and illustrations, then you receive a hardcopy of all of the work combined. They just ask that you send home order forms to students' parents. So, obviously, you need to decide if you're comfortable with that. They offer different templates to choose from depending on your grade level. This is a great way to incorporate project-based learning in your classroom!

FlipSnack
This free resource doesn't provide your students with a hardcopy of their book, but if you're okay with digital only, this site is awesome. At no charge, it converts PDF files into an interactive e-book. Students can customize the overall look of the book, and then flip through pages on their device. The teacher can view and share with other students, or choose to embed it on the class site.

DIY
Many teachers are on a strict budget, and your school probably has all the tools you need. Take advantage of the spiral binding machine and laminator. Surprisingly, laminators are actually not too expensive. If it's easier, just get one of your own!

Lulu Jr.
If you're a homeschool teacher or just want a fun project to do with your child, LuLu Jr. provides children with the opportunity to write, illustrate, and publish their very own book with their bookmaking kit. Students create the book, you send it in to be printed, and then in a few weeks they'll receive their very own professional book.

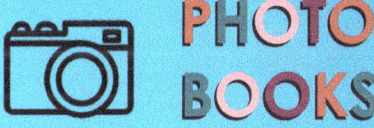

PHOTO BOOKS

There are many situations inside and outside the classroom where you may want to print your own photos as a collection.

Vacations? Birthday parties? Day-to-day life? Pictures can capture so many memories.

Chatbooks
This one you can easily do straight from your phone. It lets you select photos from your Facebook or Instagram profiles, as well as your phone's photo albums. It's straight-forward and only takes a few minutes. You can choose just one photo book, or select an ongoing series.

Print Studio
Print Studio is the way to go if you want high-quality photos or have panoramic pictures. They offer a variety of sizes and finishes for your photos, as well as a hardcover or softcover binding.

Shutterfly
You may be feeling a little more creative and opt for this site. Here, you can get more artistic and customize each page with backgrounds, designs, text, and more.

Snapfish
Snapfish is probably the most budget-friendly choice. It allows you to choose your own layouts and captions, and they always look modern and fresh.

PRO TIP: Decide which photo book printing service you're interested in, sign up for their emails and wait for a discount code. They offer discounts fairly often, and you can usually get a photo book for a very affordable price!

SCHOOL YEARBOOK

Do you run the yearbook team and need a more efficient, cost effective plan?

The internet will give you plenty of options to choose from, but don't worry; we're here to help you narrow it down. Choosing the best yearbook company can be a big decision. Figure out your budget, and then decide which one is the right fit:

Google Slides
(Followed by a Printing Company)
If you're looking for the most cost-effective route, this is the way to go. Students can design their own yearbook pages in Google Slides. Instead of paying for expensive software, the only price you need to worry about is the printing. For this, you can talk to your district office and see if they can print for you. If not, you need to look at companies that will print large quantities for you, like Blurb and Gorham Printing.

School Annual
(by Jostens Publishing)
This company is simple, and has been chosen by thousands of elementary schools. It's still appropriate for middle and high school, as well. You choose the cover and page templates, and add photos.

Entourage Yearbooks
This company is both cost-effective and high-quality. They use award-winning, innovative software to help you design your yearbook pages. Customers have emphasized it is user-friendly, and they love the availability of help if needed.

PASSION PROJECT

If you have an amazing idea for a children's book, textbook, workbook, or novel, you are not alone (especially in the world of education)!

Many teachers are already very knowledgeable about children's books, curriculum, and teen novels. There have probably been moments where you have had an idea, and thought, That'd be a really great idea for a book!

Ingramspark
The site Ingramspark is popular for self-publishing for a reason. It's main goal is to guide books from publishing houses to retailers, but they also own an amazing print on demand company that prints books all around the world, called Lightning Source. If you're looking to build a business with your book, Ingramspark is a great option, because most book retailers require this publisher.

Lulu Publishing
This company is one of the top self-publishing companies for a reason. It's free to self-publish, but you also have to take production and distribution into account. There have been negative complaints about the substantial cuts they take of author royalties. So, keep that in mind if you're hoping to make a profit off of your new book.

MindStir Media Publishing
This option is awesome if you want all the help available to self-publish. They offer services like book editing, custom book design, printing, ebook conversion, distribution, marketing, and publicity.

Kindle Direct Publishing
We all know the enormous consumer reach Amazon has in today's world. That's why their publishing services are often the first place people consider when choosing where to self-publish. They offer competitive royalties and can market your book to their millions of users. They have a KDP select program, which ties you to Amazon exclusively but offers enticing promotions. Depending on your publishing goals, this could be a great option.

PRO TIP: When you finally export your finished book to a site like Ingramspark, Lulu, etc., order just one copy. You're going to want to buy a bunch, but trust me; you're going to develop a new respect for editing. Many of us are accustomed to editing a digital product, whether that be an email newsletter, blog post, or Instagram caption. However, you can't go back and edit a printed book. Order a single copy, make sure everything is to your liking, submit changes, and then order as many copies as your heart desires!

Next Steps

PICTURE IT....

What You Need to Know to Illustrate Your Book (Legally)

GET AN ILLUSTRATOR

Today, it's easier to connect with an illustrator than ever before. First, think through everyone you know, including family, friends, and acquaintances. Do you know any artists or anyone who has a drawing or painting hobby? Ask them first if you think it could be a good fit. Not only does this show support for the individual, but it can create a more personal and meaningful end product. Depending on their level of expertise it could also be much more budget-friendly.

If you'd prefer an outside hire, determine what you're willing to pay, and begin browsing online.

Professional Online Portfolios
Gather some inspiration. Sites like ChildrensIllustrators.com and the Society of Children's Book Writers and Illustrators (scbwi.org/illustrators-gallery/) offer professional showcases of today's best children's book illustrators. They want to make it easier to source illustrators for you. Even if you don't want to hire a professional, it's worth your time to go to their website and browse the portfolios to gain inspiration and ideas. There are some seriously talented artists out there!

Freelancing Platforms
Sites like Upwork, Guru, and Fiverr allow you to hire freelance workers for a specific job. This could be conducive to a low budget depending on your preferred level of expertise.

Creative Crowdsourcing Sites
Sites such as 99designs and DesignCrowd give you the opportunity to connect with individual designers and set up contests to find the best fit for you. They are low-risk, so if you don't like any designs you don't have to pay anything at all. You fill out a brief explaining what you're looking for, the timeline, and how much you would pay a designer. Designers

submit their work, and then you pick your favorite design. The winning designer is given the prize money. Although DesignCrowd is a little less expensive, you should still be prepared with at least a few hundred dollars in your budget.

DIY

Whether you have a strict budget, you're on the artistic side, or you're just creating the book for personal use, opting for DIY illustrations could be right for you. You can do watercolor, sketching, use collage, etc; the options are endless when it comes to creating your own pages.

You could even illustrate digitally, using special software and a tablet. Do a quick YouTube Search on "How to get started with digital art" and you'll see the tools you need to be successful.

STOCK PHOTOS

When you want to use stock photos in your published book, and not your own photos, you have to proceed with caution. Basically, any photo you will find on the internet has copyrights, meaning it's illegal to use the graphic for anything other than personal use. Some images that you download from a free stock photo site have a standard license, royalty free, meaning you are protected under the terms and conditions of the stock photo agency. Google images from the internet do not carry these licensing protections. However, there are some awesome sites with millions of free stock photos and images, including Pexels, Unsplash, Pixabay, and Stock.Snap.io.

unmasking
MATH ANXIETY

It can wear many disguises...

...some of which even fool math teachers

Brigid Danziger
and Kelly Barendt
mathgiraffe.com

Suddenly, there is an overwhelming fear. Your hands start to tremble. Your heart beats rapidly. You feel your blood pressure rising. Your palms become clammy and your body starts sweating.

This is anxiety. Most individuals experience a small amount of anxiety in life, but others are less fortunate and experience it on a regular basis. Math anxiety is a form of fear and overload that commonly affects many people, both adults and children.

Where in the body do you feel anxiety? Imagine your own deep fears right now, and be aware of the physical tension. Where does it build up for you? For some, it appears as a stomachache. Other people get tense in the jaw or start to feel a headache coming on. I personally hold tension in my shoulder blades lately. My upper back muscles get so tight until I notice how much tension I am holding between my shoulder blades. By then, it is too late, and has spread to my neck and head. I have to make a point to physically relax my body to prevent it becoming a migraine.

For us, it probably does not show itself because of math problems. We have plenty of other reasons for the tension to accumulate. But we can use those experiences of feeling anxiety to relate to students who feel this in our classroom each day.

Some kids instantly feel nausea and begin to mentally shut down the moment they enter the math classroom. Some have become experts at hiding or redirecting their math anxiety as a defense.

As math teachers, it is our job to help our students overcome this math anxiety! The problem is that first, we have to spot it. This can be trickier than it seems. Students can be experts at masking their true feelings. It can be months before a teacher catches what's really going on. Some kids or teens can sneak their way through an entire year fooling their teacher into thinking that their aloof attitude, disruptive behavior, or negativity is a behavior-related issue, while in fact they are disguising their discomfort.

Officially, math anxiety is a form of anxiety that pops up specifically when a person is asked to do math. It's much more than just a dislike for the subject. Some stats say that this math-specific anxiety affects nearly half of elementary students. Unfortunately, the number of occurrences increases even beyond that as children get older.

According to *Frontiers in Psychology*, "People have been expressing mathematics anxiety for centuries. The verse 'Multiplication is vexation, and practice drives me mad' goes back at least to the sixteenth century. From a research perspective, the construct has been an important topic of study at least since the concept of 'number anxiety' was introduced by Dreger and Aiken (1957), and has received increasing attention in recent years, in conjunction with the generally increased focus on mathematical performance."

Math Anxiety Robs Working Memory

According to a fascinating article from the University of Chicago in their series *Ask a Cognitive Scientist*, a growing amount of research shows that math anxiety robs people of their mental working memory. Working memory is kind of like a scratch pad. It's where you keep several things in mind simultaneously. Without it, we couldn't problem solve and complete multiple tasks.

Working memory "space" varies from person to person, and it is required for solving math problems. So, since this anxiety creeps in when doing math, it makes sense that people with math anxiety have less room for working memory. "Anxious thoughts consume valuable working memory space...As a result, [students with math anxiety] have less working memory space to devote to the math, and their math performance suffers."

If you're wondering which of your students experience math anxiety, it may not be as obvious as it seems. Some signs to look for are avoidance, anger, lack of response, tears or discouraged attitudes, underachievement, negativity, or annoyance.

Common Causes

The first step is noting the common causes. Actually, there are quite a few common causes of math anxiety. It can help to narrow it down to a source so we can guide our students to overcome it. According to Oxford Learning, some leading causes of math anxiety are timed tests, public embarrassment, and influence of teachers.

If you do use timers when assessing students, consider other options. Could you lower the stress level in the room by allowing each student to work at her own pace?

Even if a classroom has a very positive culture, and you as the teacher know that students should not be embarrassed to give a wrong answer, some students will still have that fear. Consider using whole-group answering tools, like individual whiteboards that they can hold up. Instead of checking homework by having students call out their answers aloud, project the solutions onto the board and allow them to each check their own paper with some privacy instead. Another great trick for helping to eliminate this fear is to have large groups of students working a problem at the board. If you want to have some practice problems shown for the class to see, allow at least 5 students to solve it simultaneously in full view instead of just one student showing work in the spotlight. You can have as much as half the class working up at the board at the same time! This allows those working in notebooks at their seats to have many samples to peek up at, and it reduces the "hot seat" effect for the student(s) working in full view.

As long as algebra is taught in school, there will be prayer in school. >> Cokie Roberts

THE DISGUISES

some of the ways students mask their math anxiety

AVOIDANCE
Some students will create any excuse not to be in math class and/or do math. This may be hard to recognize in some math-anxious students who have become adept at making it seem like they are busy writing, when they're really hardly doing any math.

"I'll just choose the easier course, or skip senior math."

ANGER
Some students respond by acting out with misbehavior or an aggressive reaction. It can look like frustration, or even like rebellion.

"I'm not going to do this! I HATE math."

LACK OF RESPONSE
Some students may become extremely stressed and unable to think clearly when asked math-related questions. Others may simply act non-responsive overall while in an environment where there may be math work, which can look like shyness or social trouble from the outside.

"I just don't know. Please don't call on me."

TEARS / DISCOURAGEMENT
A student who gets easily discouraged when learning new math concepts may not even realize that he's masking an anxious reaction.

"It's just too hard. I can't do it. I need help."

UNDERACHIEVEMENT
A resistance toward math can lead a student to underachieve. They may discount it as not being as important as other subjects since it is hard for many people, or they may just have a mental block. This one is challenging especially because their poor grades only verify their beliefs about math. It can turn into a vicious cycle.

"I don't care about that low grade. It's just math, which I never do well in."

NEGATIVITY
Whether it's spoken aloud, or comes as mental self-talk, a negative attitude toward the work can be rooted in math anxiety.

"I'll never get this. I'm so bad at math."

ANNOYANCE
Acting like math is a ridiculous and unnecessary pursuit can be a very common mask for math anxiety. Some students may try to justify why it's just pointless for them to even bother with mathematics by treating it as an annoying, but non-critical part of their studies.

"This is WAY too much work for one day. Why do we need to learn this? I'll never need it."

When it comes to the factor of the teacher's own attitude, many educators think they are fine. However, you can unknowingly contribute to the problem by expressing negativity about math in a roundabout way. You may be careful not to use obvious negative talk, but there are still plenty of subtle ways that a teacher can give a negative spin to math without realizing it. Avoid comments like "Ok, this is a super easy one today," because even that may make some students feel more anxious if they don't get it right away. They'll feel more pressure. Try not to talk as if math is a higher stakes subject either. Sometimes, a deeper look at your words will help you see a student's perspective more clearly.

How to Help

Luckily, there are plenty of ways to help our students overcome math anxiety. Once you've narrowed down the common causes, try these ideas to help your students.

Use Positive Reinforcement

Since a common cause of math anxiety is public embarrassment, try eliminating disapproval or negative feedback in math class. Reward students for excellent behavior, well-thought out answers, or even extraordinary effort. Just having a relaxed atmosphere, positive classroom environment, and patience goes a long way. The more that your students feel comfortable and at home, the more their anxiety will ease up its grip.

Give Students Time to Understand

Provide students enough time to truly understand math concepts, instead of doing drilling procedures too soon. Students need a chance to develop conceptual understanding to develop joy in math! Add a step in between guided learning and practicing on their own. By bridging the two with a more supported practice, you'll decrease the anxiety levels. Offer long in-class practice sessions with your full support, walking around to assist even those who don't ask for help. This will keep them from feeling that you are throwing them into the angst of solo practice before they're ready.

Reframe Anxiety

Try having a student write down his or her worries about math before doing it. By thinking critically students can realize their fears aren't accurate. After jotting down the feeling on a sticky note, they can physically relax the part of the body where they are holding tension while they put it aside, take a deep breath, and jump in to try a problem.

Model this by sharing with your classes how you hold your own anxiety. Allow each child to reflect on their physical reaction to stress, their physical reaction to school, and then their physical reaction to math specifically. Sometimes, they are even masking the anxiety from their own awareness. They may need your assistance to even spot what is going on in their own mind.

Next, help your students see tests and quizzes as challenges, rather than a threat to their grade. Reframing how they see math can improve their fears. Offering test corrections can relieve some stress, because students know they can move on and have success. A good guideline is to give 50% of the points they would have earned if they had gotten it right the first time around. Allow plenty of time and support for the test correction process. It really encourages students to persevere instead of throwing that unit in the trash and moving on (essentially giving up on learning those concepts). I like to allow a full week for corrections, and I even believe in letting students get support from whoever they are most comfortable with, whether it's a peer, a tutor, a teacher, a sibling, or a parent. However, they need to write a full explanation for each problem, outlining the mistake, where the confusion was, and how to correct it.

Offer opportunities for meditative practices (built in!)

Swap out your active brain breaks for more meditative brain breaks. When I taught high school Geometry in a Catholic school, I loved beginning each class period with 3 minute video retreats. We prayed together, took deep breaths, and settled in. This meditative transition helped to forget the stresses of the hallway and outside world and refocus and relax our brains.

Students also enjoy chances to color. This can be a meditative practice that integrates smoothly into the learning process. I believe in fitting this in right alongside the learning goals that are already in place for each day's lesson. Doodle notes, sketch notes, and graphic organizers all offer ways for students to get the therapeutic benefits of coloring and doodling while still learning the material. This has been proven to activate the parts of the brain that help a student relax, focus, and retain the material. It will take their minds off of the stress and physically relax them! There is a reason that coloring books are becoming a therapeutic trend. The brain benefits are so easy to build into a class period! As you look at your own lesson plans, identify some places where you can incorporate some color coding, colored hand-lettering for key words, or other creative approaches. When students are able to produce something with their own creativity, they naturally relax and then can learn more effectively.

Encourage Positivity

Last, but certainly not least, teachers need to show excitement and positivity when it comes to math. Our attitudes rub off on our students, so even if math isn't your favorite subject, keep your words and actions in mind.

TIP:
Check in with other teachers. How does the student behave in ELA, or in specials? If the student that another teacher describes sounds vastly different than the child you see in math class, stress over the math itself could be the reason.

BUILDING CLASSROOM COMMUNITY

by Elizabeth Ingram

There has been an emphasis on the importance of a positive classroom community for years. It's not hard to believe that students are more likely to thrive in a place where they feel safe and loved. However, you can know that a healthy environment is crucial and still be at a loss when it comes to creating one.

How do we build classrooms that make our students feel like they can unapologetically succeed, fail, and be the best versions of themselves? How do we accomplish this when we have inevitable barriers such as varying languages, cultures, and backgrounds?

It's important to understand that there is no one-plan-fits-all when you're building classroom community. Everything should be based on the students in front of you, and oftentimes you have to get to know them as a group before you jump into a predetermined plan. You also have to be willing to modify your environment even if the same things worked wonders for your kids the previous year. Never sacrifice a positive classroom culture because you want so badly for something like flexible seating to work. It might not work, and it's okay to throw in the towel in order to meet your kids' needs.

All of that being said, there are certain things that you can implement at the beginning of the year to help your students understand that they're part of the classroom family. Start off not by telling the kids what the classroom expectations are but allowing them to have a voice in the construction of those expectations. You'd be surprised with what they come up with. Take a survey to see what authors or series they enjoy reading, and surprise them by bringing those titles into your classroom library. Spend time letting them create a classroom playlist. Explore the holidays that their families celebrate. Incorporate their native languages in your call-and-responds. You want them to be reminded constantly that they are seen and have a voice at the table.

When we're talking about getting students to feel like they're truly part of the community in the classroom, we can't overlook a teacher's powerful role. A teacher is the biggest influencer. We set the tone for the day and ultimately the year that their students will have. It's a huge responsibility to ensure that students' social and emotional needs are being met. The great news is that kids simply need to know that you care about them. Teachers often say that we don't have enough time, so it says a lot when you spend such a precious commodity to build relationships with your students. Ask them about their family and let them share their culture. Invest in your classroom community by giving your students time to discuss their life with you.

Probably the most challenging things to think about when building classroom community are the barriers that your students might face. Sometimes it's their home situation or maybe they joined us in the middle of the year. Most often, it's a language barrier in my class. I teach fourth grade in a dual language setting. I have a mixture of native English speakers and native Spanish speakers, and they all have varying amounts of proficiency in their second language. So when I plan to have these wonderful moments and share-outs during class or morning meeting, I have to take into consideration that some of my students don't yet have the vocabulary to feel successful when they're responding. It feels like walking a tightrope between pushing them to challenge themselves academically and understanding when they're uncomfortable.

You want to bring in tools and strategies to help your students navigate any barriers they have. Things like sentence starters, visual vocabulary cards, or a bilingual partner help in my case. However, I think it's okay to say that no matter how many tools you provide, each student will experience a moment of failure or embarrassment in class. When that happens, your classroom community and comradery is the net that catches them. If their environment enables them to feel safe, it will encourage them to try again and again until they find success.

Create Your Own

Custom

Wardrobe

Sara Langlier
>> High School French Teacher
>> Vintage Button Collector
>> Garment Crafter

@shadowboxworkshop
shadowboxdecor.com

Start us off with your WHY. What led you to prioritize sewing your own custom wardrobe pieces?

For me, sewing is more than just a hobby. It's a way of connecting to myself and others. It's a skill and practice that focuses me and allows me to shut everything else out. As a teacher and as a mother to two school-aged children, I always have something (or someone) pulling at me, so creating is a way for me to carve out space for myself.

Because sewing takes a lot of concentration, it forces me to slow down and pay attention to one thing. It slows my breathing down and becomes almost meditative, like running or yoga. I also love sharing my makes on Instagram and connecting with other garment-sewers through that platform. I've met so many cool people and we cheer each other on.

Can you share the specifics of your educator journey and your priorities as a teacher so far?

I'm just finishing up my nineteenth year of teaching high school French in a suburb of Boston. I have been at the same school for my whole career and I have no plans to leave! I work with incredibly supportive colleagues who are like a second family to me. My students are hardworking, kind, and engaged.

Often when I say I teach high school, people say something like, "Oh, teenagers that must be tough...," but I love teenagers. I sometimes feel like I still am a teenager (although I'm very far away from that time in my life!)

In terms of priorities, I strive to create a classroom environment where students are relaxed and having fun. I try to keep the class in French for at least 90% of class time. We talk about universal themes like the environment, friendship, and technology and have rich discussions. Right now, during COVID, I realize more than ever how lucky I am to have a job that I love. I miss my students terribly. My weekly Zoom classes are an inferior substitute for face-to-face contact.

You have so many cool things available on your website! Tell us a bit about how you make everything and run an entire crafty side gig.

My creative hobbies have gone through many iterations. Around five years ago, I started making modern collages out of paint chips from the hardware store, then I got into collecting and framing vintage buttons, and then I bought a new sewing machine and my interest in sewing was reignited! I started by making home decor such as bunting banners, coasters and pillows. I created a website and little business called Shadowbox Decor. I sold some things at craft fairs and on Etsy, but I realized I didn't love the selling aspect of all of it.

One good thing that came out of Etsy was that someone asked me to create a banner with a message on it. I didn't know how to do appliqué at the time, but I watched some tutorials and figured it out. After that, I made a number of pillows with names or images on them. Then came garment sewing, and that's pretty much all I sew now!

Give us your favorite background details about yourself. Share the basics and also some fun, different, and interesting tidbits that make you you!

I started learning French in 6th grade. In high school, it was definitely not my strongest subject. In fact, when I became a French teacher, my best friend – whom I've known since middle school – said, "But you used to cry over French!"

In college, I really fell in love with the language and culture when I studied in Paris. I ended up living in France after college for 10 months. When I returned to the States, I didn't know what to do with my life.

I worked in the corporate world briefly, but when I ended up substitute teaching in a charter school, I realized that I loved being in the classroom. I applied for a Masters program, received my teaching license, and landed a job in the school where I currently teach!

I have taken several trips to France with students. A few years ago, I established a partnership with a school in Montpellier, in the south of France. I've done two exchanges with this school and was supposed to go in April with 18 students, but then COVID happened.

What strategies help you carve out the time to create?

The nice thing about sewing clothing is that it can be broken down into many smaller steps. One day I can trace a pattern, the next day cut fabric, and then sew up a few seams after the kids are asleep. In normal times, I also take a weekly sewing class, which gets me out of the house. It's a class where we all work on our own projects, just a dedicated time each week when I can work on my craft.

What first got you interested in your crafty hobbies?

I've always taken art classes and loved doing crafty projects. I come from an artistic family, my mother was an interior designer and my sister went into the same field. Growing up, we used to love going to vintage shops to search for treasures. Seeking out funky items was a creative adventure that we all loved. That could be where my interest in design and fashion started.

How did you get started with making your own clothing?

I learned to sew over 20 years ago when I was living in New York. I wasn't happy in my corporate job and I needed to do something creative. So I signed up for sewing classes. I started making simple garments and I loved it. I would sit at my sewing machine for hours, barely getting up to eat. Even though I loved it, I never advanced my skills beyond the beginner level, and I found many of the patterns confusing. Also, my little machine was constantly jamming or sewing wonky stitches.

Fast forward to four years ago when a neighbor who is an avid quilter encouraged me to buy a new machine. That changed everything! About a year into sewing home decor items, I decided I wanted to make a simple shift dress. I was so intimidated, but I did it and wore the dress proudly.

Since then, I've discovered the world of independent sewing patterns. There are so many cool pattern companies out there now that didn't exist when I was in my twenties. They have clear instructions and make sewing such a pleasure. And of course now, anytime I'm unsure how to do something, I just turn to YouTube. Because there are so many more resources now for the home sewist, it's made it much easier to grow my skills.

What advice do you have for creative souls who have busy lives?

Carve out a little time each week that is just for you. It might mean you have to get up super early in the morning, or negotiate with a partner for that time, but you can make it happen. Schedule it and put it in the calendar!

What do most people not realize about sewing your own clothing?

I think the biggest myth is that sewing your own clothing is less expensive than buying clothes. There are definitely ways of cutting cost, like buying thrifted fabric or refashioning items you already own. But if you are buying unique, high quality fabrics, there's a cost associated with that.

Also, a big part of sewing is ironing! It's an essential step if you want your garments to look professional.

Share your favorite teaching hack or trick.

I try to get students up out of their seats as much as possible because they sit for so much of the day. I'll give them a sheet of questions and they have to find the answers around the room. It's like a scavenger hunt.

Share your favorite clothing hack or trick.

Generally, I like really simple clothing, and I mostly wear solids or stripes. But you can transform an outfit with accessories, like red shoes, a bandana, or a chunky necklace.

As I said, I love vintage buttons. I have bags of them that I pick up at thrift stores. When I find a really unique one I make it into a pin. They look great on the lapel of a blazer or on a jean jacket.

What fills your soul?

Watching family shows with my husband, kids, and dog, spending time with my best friend of over 30 years, running an after-school sewing club with my students, reading in bed, traveling to France, taking walks in the fall when the leaves have turned, listening to podcasts, and much more.

Tell us about a mentor or teacher that impacted you.

I have been lucky to have worked with several world language department heads who have been extremely supportive of me. When I started teaching, I was so green, but my department head believed in me and cheered me on. I have worked under four department heads and I consider them all mentors.

What advice do you have for the teachers of the world?

If you are a new teacher, go easy on yourself. The first few years are difficult, but as you grow as a teacher, you gain confidence and grow your arsenal of resources. You find your own style. It takes time to develop that, and it has to be authentic. Any time I tried to imitate another teacher's way of relating to students, it just felt wrong.

I'm about to enter my 20th year of teaching, and I'm still learning all the time. I used to try to make something up on the spot if a student asked me a question I didn't know the answer to. Now I'm comfortable admitting I don't know, and usually we figure it out together. It's good to show students that we are all lifelong learners.

What is your favorite book right now?

I just finished reading *This is All I Got* by Lauren Sandler. The book explores economic and racial inequities in America as it follows a young homeless mother through her son's first year of life. The woman at the center of the book is whip-smart and savvy, but she struggles in a broken system while trying to raise her son and earn her college degree.

What do you listen to? Share your favorite music picks.

I listen to a lot of podcasts. I geek out every Tuesday to the *Love to Sew* podcast. Other favorites are *Terrible, Thanks for Asking*, NPR's *Invisibilia*, *Modern Love*, and *How I Built This*.

Tips

for getting started sewing your own clothes

1 >> Start with simple patterns, like boxy tops and elastic waist skirts and pants. So many people jump right in with a complicated pattern, and that can lead to frustration. I love the shift top and dress by *Wiksten Patterns* and the Cielo Top by *Closet Case Patterns*. Another favorite is the Toaster Sweater by *Sew House Seven* patterns.

2 >> Follow hashtags for patterns you like on Instagram for inspiration and sewing advice. I've found the Instagram sewing community super helpful and welcoming.

3 >> Turn to Youtube! There are so many tutorials out there.

4 >> Take a class. It's as much about learning a new skill as it is about socializing with people who share your hobby.

5 >> Reach out to other people who sew. Other than sewing, there's almost nothing I like more than talking about sewing! I reached out to a woman I met on Instagram and it turns out she lives five minutes from my house. We went on a walk and shared our favorite patterns and sewing tips. We couldn't stop talking!

STRENGTHENING *relationships* THROUGH *renovation*

Brittany Jeltema
@thesuperheroteacher
Photography by Nicole Conner
www.nicoleconner.com

Sometimes, what it takes to get the culture and connections just right is an overhaul of the physical space.

Expert classroom renovator Brittany Jeltema shares how small steps toward revamping different areas in your own classroom can lead to healthier, happier relationships.

What do most people not realize about your work transforming learning spaces?

The classroom flips I do are so much more than just pretty classroom decor. They are purposeful and designed WITH the teacher and students in mind. Before my team and I step foot in the classroom, I have several meetings with the teacher and administration to ensure that I'm designing a space that they truly want and need-- an environment that will match their teaching style.

What fills your soul?

Seeing the reactions of teachers and students when I show them their new space is why I give back the way I do. When they open their eyes for the first time and I see their faces light up, it's impossible not to be filled with joy! My favorite part of the process is when they walk around the classroom and start talking to themselves… they begin thinking and sharing how the space is going to change and improve their classroom environment and relationships, and that kind of impact is truly what fills my soul.

Tell us about a mentor or teacher who inspired you.

When I was in high school, my family was experiencing an extremely challenging time. I could have easily gone down the wrong path at this point. I truly felt like I had nowhere to turn. However, when I would enter my sophomore English class, I knew that I would be greeted by Coach Flores. She was the teacher that didn't let me fall through the cracks. She called me out into the hallway and was the first person to ask if I was okay and how she could help. Through incoherent sobs, I managed to explain what was going on and from that day forward, she helped me, guided me, and checked in on me. She probably doesn't realize it, but she is the reason I'm a teacher today. I knew I wanted to have that lasting impact on students as well.

MEET

Ever since I started my career in the world of education, my WHY has been centered around reaching as many teachers and students as possible and have a positive, lasting impact.

I've always loved anything related to interior design and graphic design! During my 4th year of teaching, I went back to grad school to get my master's degree in marketing. It was during this time that I truly learned the importance of design, environment, and color psychology. I realized that our classrooms need to be MARKETABLE to our students.

If we walked into a grocery store to buy food and everything was a disaster or horribly organized or distractedly busy to the point where we couldn't focus, we would immediately leave, and the same should apply to our classroom and bulletin boards! I wanted to help teachers design in a way that appeals to their students — like an advertisement to entice learners — and create in a way that students want to BUY IN to their atmosphere and curriculum.

As a way to give back to teachers, I hosted a giveaway on Instagram for a classroom makeover. I had no idea what I was doing, but I knew I wanted to help a deserving teacher design the environment of their dreams! My team and I traveled 870 miles to a school in Minnesota and flipped a deserving teacher's classroom. The reaction of the teacher in response to her space was such an adrenaline rush for me. I knew I needed and wanted to help more teachers. Since then, I've completed 12 classroom makeovers with my incredible team.

After communicating extensively with the teacher and getting everything approved by administration, we go into the classroom and work tirelessly until everything is perfectly in place! Often times, we will work from 6am to 9pm for four days straight. A few times, we've experienced hiccups and didn't leave the classroom until 3am! Regardless of the time we leave, every member of my team has the same goal, and that's to give a deserving educator a beautiful, meaningful space to watch their students grow.

These classroom renovations are my absolute passion. Helping teachers create an environment that is safe and inclusive for every student that enters their classroom has fulfilled that passion of mine, which is why I continue flipping classrooms!

How do you balance work and life?

I learned the hard way that focusing on mental health is, without a doubt, the most important component to finding that stability. Limiting time on social media, traveling with my amazing wife, and spending time with friends and family has allowed me the freedom to have energy and time to focus on creating curriculum and designing classrooms.

ENVIRONMENT SHIFT #1

visible collaboration

Student-Teacher Teamwork is Enhanced Through Interactive Decor Features

FLIP TIP: A fresh coat of paint can transform a space on a limited budget. Usually, on the first day of the makeover, we paint the walls. It creates a huge impact and it won't break the bank! My favorite color (that I've used in every single classroom makeover) is Ultra Pure White by Behr.

By using collaborative seating and interactive bulletin boards, this space provides teachers AND students the opportunity to work together and develop a sense of team work.

This classroom renovation was in Monument Valley, Utah on the Navajo Reservation. I wanted to create an inviting and innovative environment for these 10th grade English students using flexible and collaborative seating around the room.

TEACHER HACK:
Use clothing hangers to display student work!

When I'm designing a new classroom renovation, I always keep both students and teachers in mind. The environment that I create will reflect the student relationships that are built with the teacher.

I could create the most beautifully designed classroom in the world, but without connections to students, it means nothing! I do my best to create an atmosphere that fosters student relationships by focusing on these four elements:

1. CREATING A SAFE SPACE
2. CLASSROOM FLOORPLAN
3. PURPOSEFUL DECOR
4. CALMING ATMOSHPHERE

ENVIRONMENT SHIFT #2

healing & peace

Students' Internal Relationships with Their Own Challenges or Trauma Transforms into Growth

5 tips for creating the perfect classroom environment:

1. Strengthen student relationships using student-teacher conferences at the beginning, middle and end of year.

2. Create a classroom atmosphere that feels safe for all students.

3. Use teamwork challenges, like creating and escaping a human knot, to create a collaborative vibe.

4. Display student work to promote student successes.

5. Use the psychology of color to create a space that fits your classroom mission and brand!

Personally, I am inspired by comfort and safety. If I feel like I'm in an environment where I'm free to be unapologetically myself, I'll open up, share more about myself, and work more productively. The same goes for our students. If students feel like they are accepted and appreciated in their space, they will respond with engagement, trust, and productivity.

This particular classroom makeover was unique because the students and staff had experienced a tragedy. My hope and goal was to provide a space that promoted healing and growth together.

TEACHER HACK: Create cozy nooks with motivational books, magazines, etc. around your classroom to create an area for students to escape when they're feeling overwhelmed!

This makeover was for an incredibly deserving teacher, Brittany Sinitch, in Parkland, Florida. She wanted a space that felt like a home away from home-- an environment where students could become family. We used farmhouse tables and non-traditional seating around the room to develop that vibe.

FLIP TIP: Use color psychology when choosing the theme of your classroom. When I was in grad school for marketing, I took an entire course on the importance of branding and what goes into the branding process and one of the key components was the psychology of color and choosing colors that fit your mission and brand! The colors you choose for your classroom reflect the personalities that will emerge from your students. While there is no right or wrong color to use in your classroom, you may be using décor that doesn't fit the mood you want to evoke in your classroom without even realizing it!

For example, if you're looking to create a serene, calm environment, but your décor is all red, orange, and yellow, you may find that your classroom is actually more energetic and spontaneous as opposed to that calm feel you're looking for.

Britt's Picks:

My go to playlists on Spotify are:
1. Pumped Pop
2. I Love my '00s R&B
3. Morning Acoustic
4. With You
5. Low-Key

My go to playlists on Pandora are:
1. Chillwave Radio
2. Bon Iver Radio
3. King Princess Radio
4. Lizzo Radio
5. Indie Folk Revival

Student-to-Student Bonds Deepen with Family Style Setups

gathering space

ENVIRONMENT SHIFT #3

This makeover took place in Cleveland, Ohio for Marguerite Haas! She wanted a sophisticated, but playful environment for her elementary students, so I designed a jungle and rainforest themed space-- filled with flexible seating, interactive photos of jungle animals around the room, and collaborative gathering areas.

By using several interactive bulletin boards and displays around the room, students and Ms. Haas are able to work together to learn and engage with the classroom decor!

ENVIRONMENT SHIFT #4

representation

Comfort Levels and Relationships Thrive when Each Student's Story is Represented

This classroom renovation was designed for the incredibly talented Layla Helwa from Philadelphia! She teaches African American History to high school students and loves utilizing art in her classroom. With that in mind, I flipped her classroom into an interactive art gallery! Each powerful piece of art in the room is paired with a QR code that links to a famous or empowering speech, quote, or article.

Giving students a classroom in which they feel represented is so important when it comes to classroom environment and design. Layla and I are both queer educators proud to represent the LGBTQ+ community. We both discussed how the lack of representation when we were in school greatly impacted our adulthood. Because of that, I find it incredibly important to represent every student in the room.

I asked Layla to share a piece about how the classroom makeover fostered relationships and this is what she said:

"The classroom makeover definitely brought out a new sense of community in my room! I felt so inspired by the art and messages in my room. I tried out a new intro to my Reconstruction unit. Students used their knowledge of race and racial constructs to tackle modern day issues and try to develop modern day solutions to them.

Students discussed healthcare, immigration, and the criminal justice system and were able to gain feedback from their peers on their solution! I think the new layout of my classroom also encourages the students to be more collaborative with their peers during their discussions. As a class we were definitely engaging with each other in new ways!

The makeover also allowed me more flexibility and ability check in with different groups of students more easily! Those standing desks are phenomenal. I could easily jump into a group and listen in to their discussion or correct their papers. Sometimes while giving instructions or reading a text as a class, I'd just set myself up at a standing desk with the kids!

As an educator, I think the biggest thing this makeover has given me is a continuous source of inspiration when designing my lessons for my kids. When I sit at my desk to plan and look at the empowering messages around me, I can't help but try to make my lessons match the room. While teaching about the beginnings of Jim Crow and the resilience of black communities across the US, I worked even harder to find unique and inspirational stories to teach my kids so that they can know that black history is full of power and brilliance.

I want my kids to know that the history that we learn in my room is important and should be a source of pride. The makeover helped me refocus myself and re-imagine what my teaching practice looked like!"

Educators are the REAL superheroes!!! I give back through classroom makeovers because teachers are changing the world every single day. When I read through the applications, I'm continuously impressed by how hard teachers are working to reach every single student that enters their classroom.

For inspiration, I'm a HUGE fan of mood boards! I create one for every classroom renovation. When I'm looking for inspiration, I look at home design magazines and websites to develop that home away from home vibe in the space. Also, interviewing the winning teacher is always super helpful. I can create an atmosphere that represents their teaching style and personality!

Over time, I have become more daring with my designs. Everything has to be approved by administration first, so I love working with teams who allow unique things in the classroom, like a large collaborative farmhouse table instead of a traditional desk or using waterproof wood flooring instead of carpet.

Every teacher is different, so every makeover is unique as well! This gives me the opportunity to challenge myself and try new things.

Also, working on a limited budget has given my team and me an opportunity to learn new skills, like installing flooring, working with power tools, and so much more!

Inspiration, Lesson Ideas, & Priorities

by Maggie @countingcures
a 2nd grade teacher who transitioned to educating her own family at home.

Insights from a Faith-Filled Teacher

"You have countless chances to teach them a math concept or spelling rule. You only have ONE shot to teach them a love of learning. So, err on the side of feeding that fire instead of burning it out."

photography by Colorado Lifestyle Photography

We just love learning about the ocean, probably because the topics are as endless as the ocean itself! We use felt sets from Twig and Daisy on Etsy all the time and love the vibrance and durability of them! We try to incorporate hands on learning as much as possible! My kids are usually more creative than I am on the project-based learning front and make suggestions such as replicating the layers of the ocean floor with play foam or mimicking the layers of ocean with different shades of blue colored water. It's amazing what those little minds can come up with!

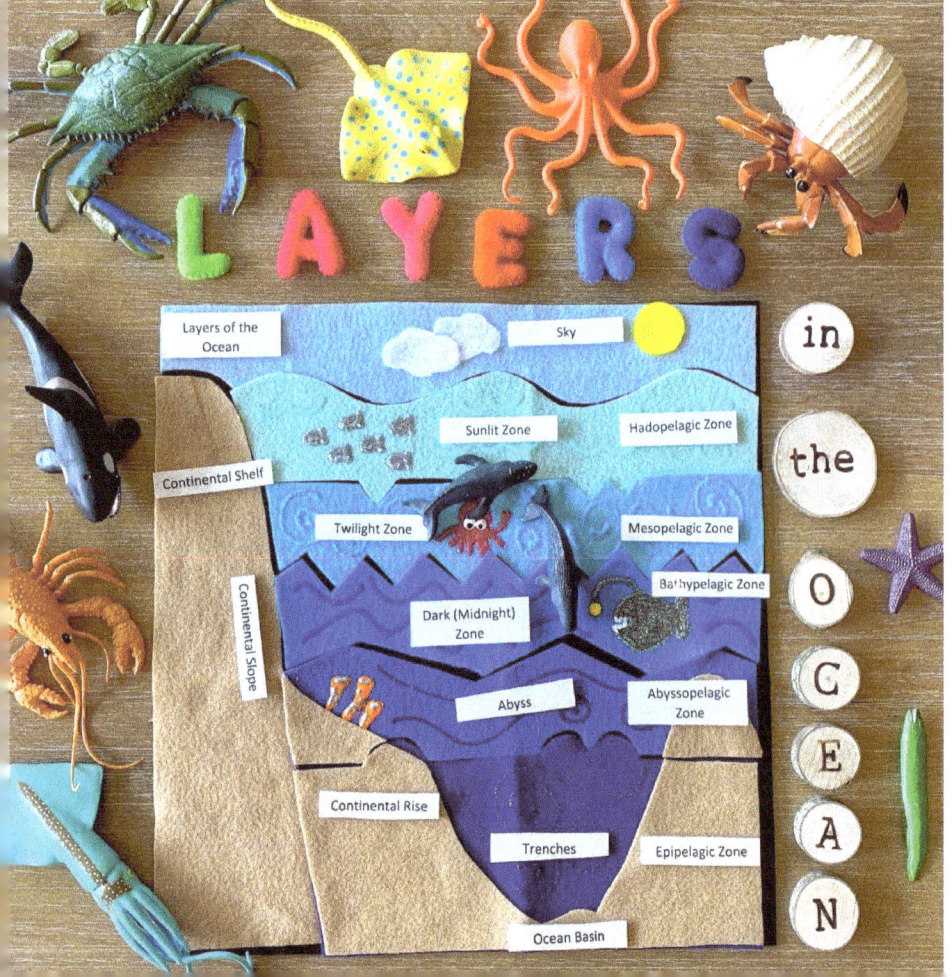

Years ago, I stumbled upon a family of high schoolers outside of church. Simply they way they met completely struck me. It was uncommon to come by such genuine teenagers. It was evident they knew their own worth as well as mine.

I thought, "I need to see what their mom is doing, because I want my kids to turn out that way!" Her family has done both homeschool and normal school. She has answered all my questions along the way, encouraged me in times of doubt, and has truly brought companionship to an area of my life that can at times seem isolating compared to what the world thinks education should look like.

Wisdom and experience are invaluable; seek them when you can!

Before giving birth to my first child, I was a 2nd grade teacher with an additional degree in early childhood education. Never had it crossed my mind that one day I might homeschool my own kids. Four babies later, here I am in the joyful, chaotic trenches of motherhood and homeschool. Once our first was getting ready to be school age, we tried to prayerfully discern what God was calling him (and us) to.

Of course, in my mind, I thought that meant public school or private school. Then came the shocking conviction of homeschool. That year so many wonderful homeschool moms were providentially placed in my life and I was able to work through all of my fears and hesitations with them. I particularly loved talking to moms who had sent their kids to school as well as homeschooled so I could get a thorough, unbiased perspective. Although I wasn't sure for how long I'd homeschool, I knew I had to give myself one year to try it and gain more clarity.

The clarity was powerfully convicting in every way I didn't expect. I was prepared to evaluate the curriculum, feel out learning styles, master our organization and schedule. I was NOT prepared for the incredible family bonds, the feeding of souls, the extensive creativity, and what adventures a classroom without four walls could bring.

I have loved being able to specifically tailor education to each of my kids' needs and desires. When certain topics are requested, we take it and run with it. Kids are naturally attracted to what is beautiful and they are naturally born to CREATE. So, we do our best to allow for creating beauty associated with what they want to learn about!

I was born and raised in Colorado and knew from childhood I wanted to be a teacher and mama! I attended Saint Mary's College in Notre Dame, IN where I met my husband over at Notre Dame. My sister and I married brothers, so it's a little too much fun when we all get together! Having babies young has been an incredible blessing in many ways and I highly recommend it to any mom if it is possible. Sometimes it's easy to fear what one will miss out on in life if you and your husband have kids right away... the kicker is you have no idea how much you ARE missing out on until you have babies.

My soul is filled by being WITH my kids. I truly love it more than anything in the world. Slowing down to their pace of life and soaking in the simple moments of these fleeting days is invigorating, despite the exhaustion. Second to being with them, having the privilege of watching them learn has been an irreplaceable gift.

Universal Keys to a Productive Learning Environment

My kids noticeably thrive in a tidy, organized, and timely environment. Having four kids, our environment isn't always described as those three words. But, I try my best to maintain order to their day and they have come to love the predictability. To ensure our learning space is nurturing, we look at education as an exciting privilege that a child gets to partake in when he is ready. We try to allow as much time for creating and exploring as possible to design an environment that truly allows them to experience the sweetest simplicities of childhood.

Keeping Perspective & Balance while Managing it All

I was one of the lucky moms who got 8 arms, so it helps a lot... kidding; I wish! No matter what, don't all of us moms feel inadequate in one way or another at the end of each day? The first key is perspective. I used to base my success on how much I could get done, and now I base it on how present I was to my children since that truly is my first job. Logistically, I use block scheduling, which I love. I run a tight ship for myself but it's really how the house functions best. Certain hours of the day are blocked off for household chores (which is a family affair), certain hours are blocked off for schooling, others for recreation, cooking, praying, etc. And the best tip I've learned is to block off 20 minutes more for each area than you think to give yourself a margin, perhaps even free time to breathe, instead of constantly feeling like you are running out of time!

"Kids are naturally attracted to what is beautiful and they are naturally born to CREATE."

Truths About Homeschool

Most people do not realize that homeschool should NOT look like standardized school. If it does, what's the point? Almost all school standards should be thrown out the window and recreated because the circumstances are starkly different, and should therefore look different.

1) YOU are now the one spending a majority of your child's childhood with him. And guess what: no one loves him OR knows him better than you do. So, already, you are made to be a better teacher for him even if you don't have a teaching degree. Pressure is off there!

2) You now have one-to-one teacher to student ratio as opposed to the typical one to twenty-five, so you shouldn't be shocked when your school day is done in 2 hours, compared to 7. Don't worry, you still covered just as much content AND tailored it to your child's learning style.

3) One curriculum doesn't fit all. The beauty of homeschool is you can adapt every lesson and subject to not only fit your child's learning style but to fit his desires.

4) Did you know studies show socialization is most successfully taught when your child spends a majority of his day around mature socializers and a minority of it trying it out on peers his age? It's amazing what a wide variety of kids, people, babies and adults your kids get to speak to when out and about on week days.

Faith, Family, and Priorities

Faith is far more important to us than education. That statement does not undermine education at all because we hold it in high regard as well, but faith is our number one. We love that homeschool enables faith to be permeated throughout all of our conversations, lessons, and parts of our day instead of compartmentalized into one subject area or saved for when kids get home from school.

Although we will get more into the depths and details of faith in the coming years, it is most important to us to LIVE it joyfully now so the kids can simply witness it and be in the presence of a strong faith. We also love focusing on weekly virtues at these young ages, because religious or not, virtues help raise good humans!

My husband and I try to live out our faith daily, so that is always present for our own kids to witness. We have tried to build friendships and have been blessed with family that both emulate the faith in a joyfully contagious manner. I believe witnessing someone's joy and hope in Christ can be far more convicting than learning it in a book. But...we still learn it in a book too! At their young ages, my kids love daily bible stories, dancing to bible songs, and just chatting with God when they have a thought or feeling on their hearts.

I LOVE my hanging-file plastic bin that stores my WHOLE year of grab and go lessons that I can carry anywhere. My smoothest years come from planning in the summer and having all my lessons ready to grab and go in that bin for the year! I go from scrambling to plan to ENJOYING learning alongside my kids when I do this.

Integrated Curriculum

Selfishly, the more I can integrate subjects the easier it is on me to not teach multiple individual subjects. The more I integrate subjects, the less the kids realize they are learning and the more they dive into the aspect of the topic that is most appealing to them. I have learned that the textbooks and lesson plans simply guide and prompt but really our conversation around the topic allows us to pull in all subjects. When reading the Hungry Caterpillar, we don't need lesson plans and separate subjects to learn the life cycle and anatomy of a butterfly, while counting fruits by 1s or 2s, while adding in the simple phonics of "B is for butterfly, b- b- butterfly" while talking about geographical migrations butterflies can take. It didn't take a geography book, science diagrams, alphabet flashcards and math manipulatives; all it took was simple conversation with a picture book!

My favorite topic is Ancient Egypt because it is my boys' favorite topic. I mean, I watch them truly come alive and lose all sense that they are learning as they giddily immerse themselves into life in Ancient Egypt. From constructing the Nile River in the back yard with a hose, to making sugar cube pyramids, to writing in hieroglyphs to mummifying each other, they have a lot of fun! The Ancient Egypt study runs right into Ancient Greece, where we create our own Olympic Games. Our best days of learning are when textbooks are closed and imaginations are open!

Embracing Technology

I think it is so important to teach technology, because our world so often depends on it. Although I think limited screen time is healthy, my kids have some of their best educational memories from incredible documentaries! I think if technology is used in moderation and wisely, it can be wonderful! I also firmly believe we have a great duty to prepare and protect our children from all of the dangers that can come from technology.

Support for Moms, Teachers, and Homeschoolers

My passion is to make even just one mom less afraid of motherhood or homeschool if she happens to have any hesitation or worry. My goal is to show the true joy that comes from motherhood and how that joy trumps all exhaustion and how in "giving up" your old life, you gain the world.

You have countless chances to teach them a math concept or spelling rule. You only have ONE shot to teach them a love of learning. So, err on the side of feeding that fire instead of burning it out.

I LOVE following teacher mamas whose educating comes second to feeding souls. Kristen @ourdarlingchaos is my go-to favorite. She's a mom to 7 babies in 8 years, all of which brought her hypermesis through pregnancy. Her account is an incredible witness to JOY through suffering and how chaos and exhaustion can lead to lasting fulfillment.

In a current world full of uncertainty, be certain of yourself, that God fully equipped you to do and be everything your child needs. Don't worry so much about the DOing and focus on the BEing. YOU are the greatest gift he or she will receive.

countingcures.com
@countingcures

> To the teachers of the world: "I cannot think of a more honorable job in the world than to care for a soul God created for more hours in a day than his or her own parent does. It's heroic, admirable, and sweetly appreciated."

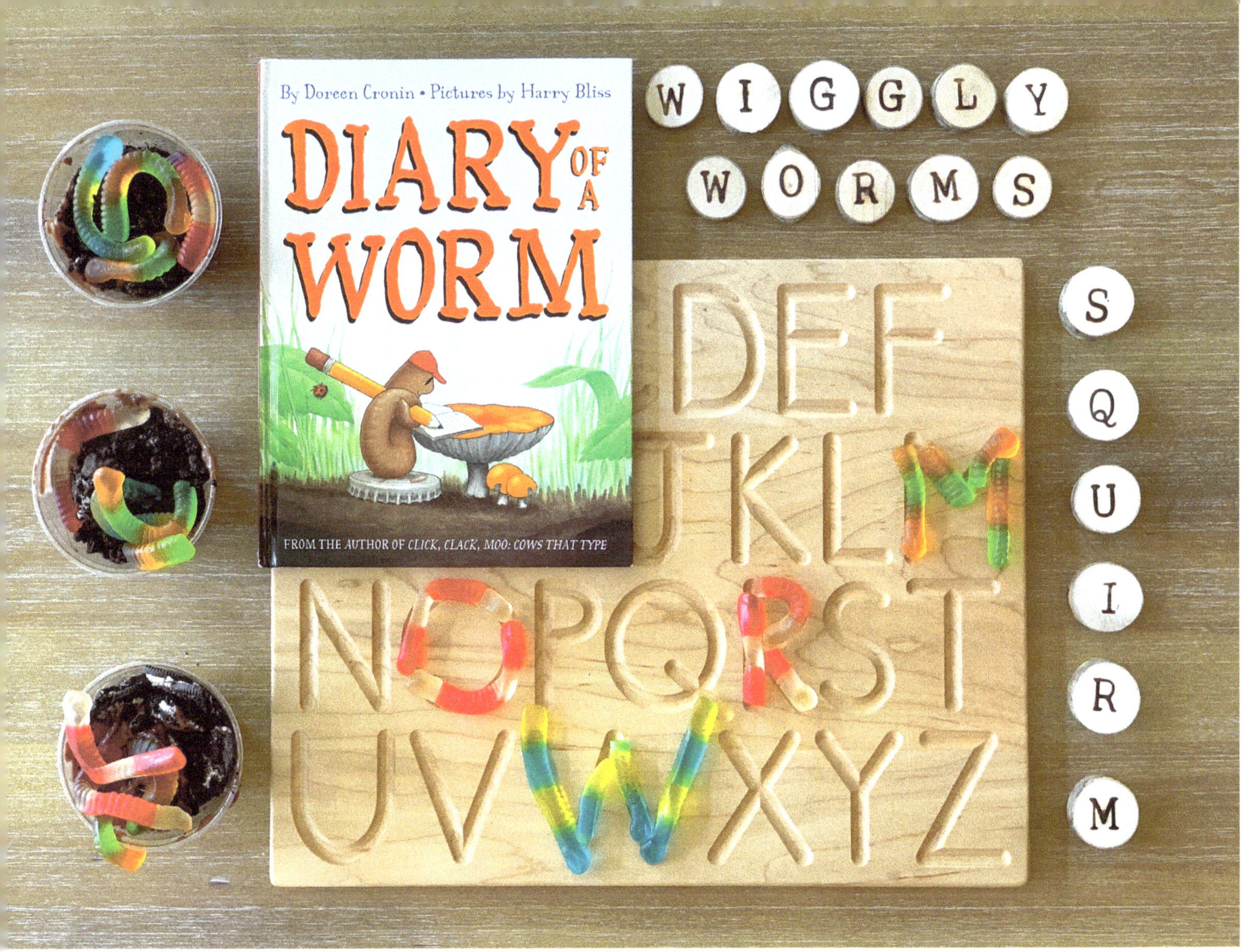
By Doreen Cronin • Pictures by Harry Bliss
DIARY OF A WORM
FROM THE AUTHOR OF CLICK, CLACK, MOO: COWS THAT TYPE
WIGGLY
WORMS
SQUIRM

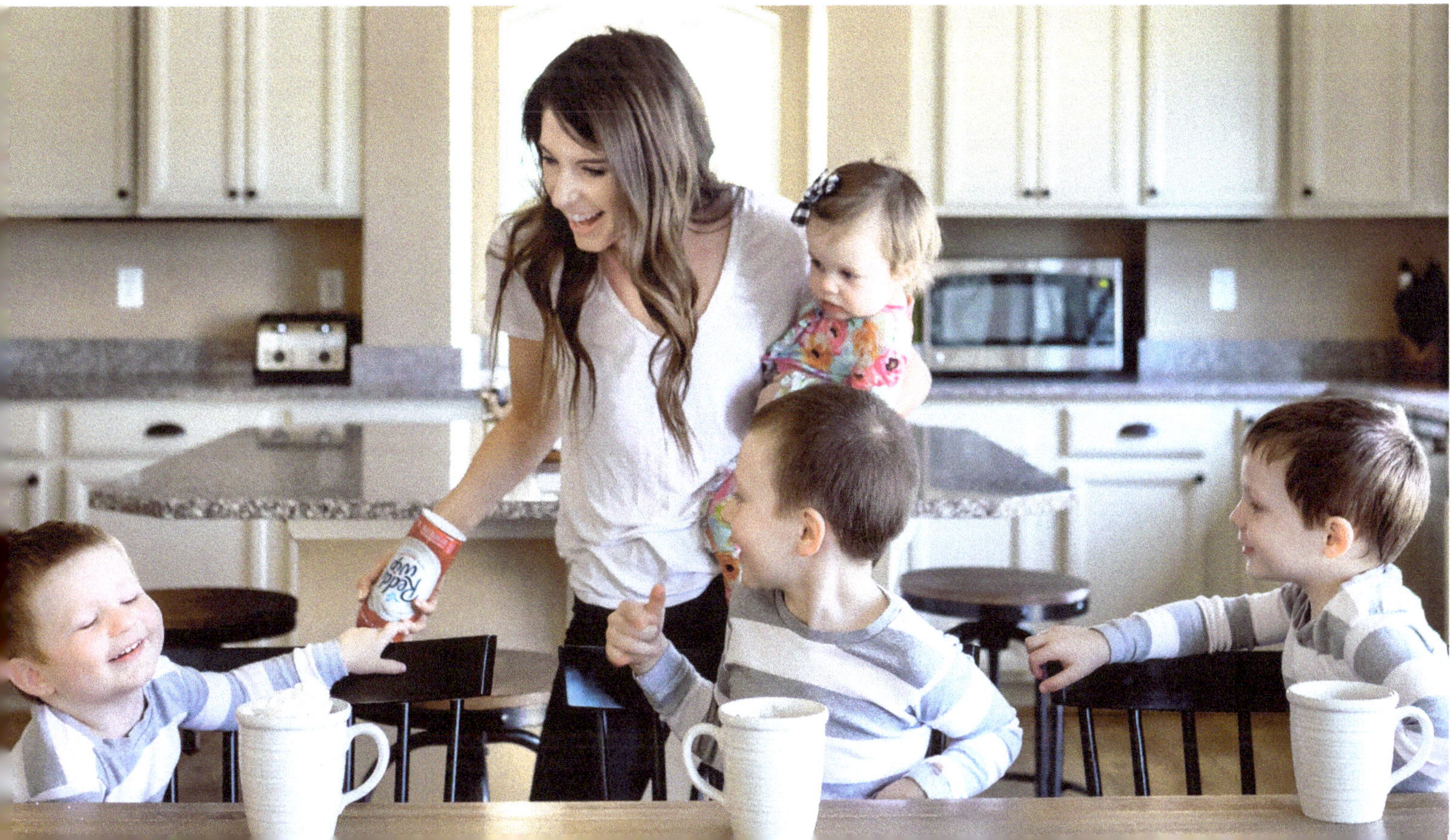

HOW TO STAY IN COMMUNICATION WITH PARENTS
(Without Giving Your Phone Number)

BY KELLY BARENDT

Positive relationships between schools and families are essential for students' success. Important (yet, not surprising) research from the Harvard Graduate School of Education in 2012 showed that everything from behavior to test scores improves when parents and teachers communicate frequently to support students. Parent-teacher communication is one of the most important factors in building relationships. We all know this communication can be overwhelming. You teach many students with parents with differing expectations and needs.

There are plenty of teachers out there who happily give out their phone number to parents. They're okay with receiving texts and phone calls at any hour of the day, or maybe their parents don't overuse this method of contact. However, it's totally okay if giving your personal number isn't for you. It's not a one size fits all situation.

BASIC STRATEGIES

There are definitely certain approaches that can greatly improve parent-teacher communication. Keep these in the forefront of your mind from the very beginning of the school year!

Partner with parents to foster success with their children. Make it a point to guide them through checking on their students' progress, as well as any class updates. For example, on Meet the Teacher night, instruct parents and families on the details of checking the class site or app you've chosen for communication. When you are working together, success is more likely to follow.

Effective communication is key, but realize that effective communication is not just a steady stream of updates and reminders; it's a two-way process that facilitates a mutually beneficial relationship. You must listen to parents, as well as inform.

Be as transparent as possible. Parents are placing a lot of faith in you to educate their children. At the start of the school year, let parents know you will inform them immediately about any concerns you might have with regard to their child.

Be consistent. Begin each year by explaining how and when you'll keep in touch with them. Then, be sure to follow through to build trust. Building trust is gradual and slow, but knowing they can count on you will greatly improve your relationship.

TIME-SAVING TRICKS

Teachers' time is too valuable to waste, especially on tasks that can easily be streamlined. Here are some time-saving tricks that can improve your parent-teacher communication while saving your sanity.

Start by checking out some of the top apps. These make parent-teacher communication feel like you're scrolling through Facebook or other social media. It's quick and easy to be in touch and give updates.

Bloomz
Bloomz is one of the best school communication apps, and it's very clear why once you start using it. It has a really easy-to-use interface that allows teachers and parents/families to easily communicate. It's like a secure Facebook for just your classroom. There are features that allow two-way messaging, classroom updates, calendar integration, and more.

Class Dojo

ClassDojo is easily one of the most beloved and popular classroom communication apps. In fact, it's being used in 90% of K-8 classrooms. It's designed to keep parents updated on what's going on in the classroom, including everything from important reminders to individual classroom management updates.

Remind

This app gives teachers the ability to send messages or reminders to an individual, a specific group, or the entire class. They aim to make communication between parents and families a breeze.

Talking Points

This app is extremely useful for teachers and parents attempting to break down language barriers. The teacher can send a message (in English) and the message can be translated into dozens of languages. The parent can respond in their native language, and it will be translated into English. It is essentially an easier, more efficient way to communicate rather than using Google Translate constantly.

Classting Social media

Classting is a free app that allows teachers, as well as parents and families, to post on a joint classroom wall. There's an individual messaging option, too. Also, this app has a cool feature where your classroom wall can be combined with any classroom around the world, making school experiences more global.

SMALL CONSISTENT STEPS

The next big tip is to always send that note, reminder, or update as soon as possible. Of course, you may be in the middle of teaching or some other all-consuming task, but you can still get the message out as soon as you get the chance. This trick saves you from adding yet another item to your to-do list. The sooner you get the message out, the sooner it's off your plate.

Email is a blessing and a curse. It's convenient to facilitate communication, but at the same time, can consume too much of your day. If you haven't read it already, use our "Inbox Hacks" article in this issue to learn some email productivity hacks, like how to make canned templates.

Use Interactive Notebooks to keep parents informed. If you already use interactive notebooks in your class, you know the effort and creativity that students put forth. A few times a year, have your students stick a chart in their notebooks with designated columns for the dates, parent signatures, and optional comments. This is an awesome way to keep parents in the know. They'll also love using it as a conversation starter.

INDIVIDUALIZED WAYS TO TOUCH BASE WITH ONE FAMILY (IF NEEDED)

From time to time, you will have a student that requires a more individual and frequent method of communication. Using a parent-teacher communication app that allows individual messaging could be the quickest and easiest way to communicate concerns or improvements regarding this child. Many teachers would recommend using something tangible; online systems are more likely to be forgotten about and might not be as consistent.

Implementing a behavior clipboard, for example, worked wonders with one first grade student. She had trouble remaining calm and quiet when needed, so she was eventually given a small clipboard with a behavior chart. For each day of the week, there were three faces- smiling, neutral, or frowning. At the end of the school day, while students were packing up, Emily had to bring her clipboard to her teacher and they would briefly discuss her behavior that day. Depending on what they determined, Emily would color in the corresponding face, and take it home for a parent to sign. The teacher collected the chart at the end of the week.

This technique worked wonderfully for Emily because it required responsibility, self-reflection, and critical thinking on her part. Depending on the student and their needs, you can adjust any of this. Maybe for teens, it'd make more sense for the student to write a self-reflection statement on their chart and require the parent to sign at the end of the week.

NEWSLETTER TEMPLATES

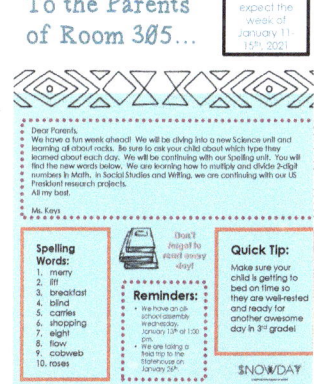

An easy way to keep continuous communication flowing is by implementing a weekly newsletter into your routine. Maybe this means taking a few minutes each Sunday to type out an email update for your students and families about what they can expect, or maybe it'd make more sense for you to send home a hard copy with your students every Friday.

Typing out a weekly newsletter might seem a little daunting, but if you put effort and thought into creating a newsletter template, it can take less than 10 minutes each week. Here's an example template. You can go to snowdaymagazine.com to download this editable template for free!

The Widespread Impact of

SLEEP

THE SURPRISING ROOT OF MANY OF OUR STUDENTS' PROBLEMS

Misdiagnosed ADHD, Depression, and other Issues Can Often Actually be Attributed to Lack of Sleep

Did you know that children in China continue midday napping through elementary school, middle school, and even into adulthood?! More sleep in children has been found to significantly improve happiness, control, and grit. Adversely, sleep deficiency can cause a number of problems, like chronic disease and behavioral problems.

Some researchers are surprised to find that many of the diagnoses our children and teens are receiving can instead be attributed to extreme sleep deprivation based on their age and needs.

We can't change our school day schedules overnight, but we can educate our students' parents about the widespread impact of a good night's sleep, as well as the negative impact of sleep deficiency.

Impact of Healthy Sleeping Habits

Every single person needs sleep every night to support their circadian rhythm, or sleep-wake cycle. Studies have found that children's mental and physical health are directly affected by sleep. Healthy and consistent sleep habits are associated with better language development, academic achievement, and socio-emotional and behavioral functioning in young children. Other studies have shown that kids of all ages who regularly get an adequate amount of sleep have improved attention, behavior, learning, memory, and overall mental and physical health.

So, how do we help children develop healthy sleep habits?

First, students need the recommended number of hours of sleep per night. Depending on their age, the numbers vary:
Infants under 1 year: 12-16 hours
Children 1-2 years old: 11-14 hours
Children 3-5 years old: 10-13 hours
Children 6-12 years old: 9-12 hours
Teenagers 13-18 years old: 8-10 hours

For teens who wake up at 6am to get on the bus, for example, this would mean getting to bed between 8 and 10pm. Is that the reality for most of your students? Not likely. But are parents and teens aware that it could be the root of their problems with weight, hormone imbalances, trouble focusing, or depression?

Beyond just the time spent in bed, it needs to be quality sleep. It's important for parents to consider bedtime routines. Consistent bedtime routines are critical for younger children, (daily, positive interactions that end with the child sleeping). Healthy bedtime routines should include things like brushing teeth and bathing, reading books together, and physical contact for younger children. They may look different for older children and adolescents as they become more and more independent, but should still be happening.

> IN THE U.S. 30% OF KIDS AND 73% OF HIGH SCHOOL TEENS DO NOT GET ENOUGH SLEEP

Parents of teens often drastically miscalculate the hours their child actually spends sleeping. They imagine them resting from the time they "clock out" for the day until the alarm goes off, but adolescents are frequently spending hours scrolling, reading, texting, or even just thinking while their caretakers assume they are asleep.

These reasons combine to cause a lot of confusion when a student starts to have trouble. Experts in pediatrics and in education both tend to look toward certain common explanations or diagnoses, when in fact, for many students, sleep should be the very first thing that is questioned.

Diagnoses that Could be Explained by Sleep Deficiency

There are many diagnosed behaviors and conditions in classrooms that could be a result of sleep deficiency. Not always, but oftentimes, students suffer from obesity or are misdiagnosed with ADHD or depression. Professionals will follow along with treatments accordingly when really, a lack of sleep might be the root cause.

The wonderful upside is that in cases where sleep is successfully identified as the root of the issue, the problem is easily solved. Working to get more rest is free of any negative side effects, and will have additional benefits for the whole child.

OUR CHILDREN AND TEENS ARE SLEEP DEPRIVED. AND WE'RE MISSING THE SIGNALS. OR WORSE, MISDIAGNOSING WHAT'S GOING ON.

ADHD

Attention-Deficit/Hyperactive Disorder is prevalent in today's schools. Millions of children have been diagnosed with ADHD in the US, and the number has only risen over the years. But, did you know that sleep deprivation and ADHD exhibit some of the exact same symptoms?

The behaviors associated with ADHD interfere with a child's social and intellectual development, which can lead to problems with relationships with other children and adults, at school and at home. But, ADHD might not always be the underlying cause.

That's right, many cases of ADHD are misdiagnosed, and forming healthy sleep habits could solve the problem. Some symptoms ADHD and sleep deprivation have in common are inattention, hyperactivity, anxiety, agitation, nervousness, insomnia, and weight loss.

Often, when a child is acting out and we don't see an obvious cause, doctors jump to an ADHD diagnosis. Sometimes, though, the child is suffering from sleep-disordered breathing, causing disruption to sleep patterns. At the NIH, they studied children with ADHD who were on medication, and fixed their sleep-disordered breathing. Within just 6 months, 70% no longer showed ADHD symptoms and could be taken off medication.

The Child Mind Institute shares, although sleep disorders are rare in children, a lack of sleep (even if it's not considered a sleep disorder) can cause or worsen ADHD symptoms. So, if a student is diagnosed with ADHD, you may want to advise parents to pay attention to any sleep disturbances, and follow up with their physician.

It's also worth noting that ADHD medication can play a role in sleep deficiency. Children who take stimulant medication might experience symptoms, like deficient sleep. If the child takes the stimulant too late in the day or if it keeps working too long, they might have trouble falling asleep. It's worth bringing up any of these concerns with your doctor.

Obesity

As you probably know, obesity is prevalent in the US. It affects about 17% of children and 35% of adults. Obesity often leads to many other medical problems, like cardiovascular disease, diabetes, and hypertension. Studies have also found it might cause sleep apnea in children.

Most people automatically jump to poor diets and exercise habits as the cause of this epidemic. Although these definitely need to be considered, poor sleep patterns are often overlooked. Most studies have shown a convincing association between a lack of quality sleep and increased weight gain in children. Different factors determine quality sleep, such as the duration of sleep at night (Is the child getting the recommended number of hours of sleep per night?), or sleep patterns (Is the child following a strict bedtime?).

As mentioned earlier, depending on their age, children and adolescents need a certain number of hours of sleep, and multiple reviews have determined there is a relationship between sleep duration and childhood obesity. The underlying explanation(s) are still unknown though. Some theorize it is because poor sleep can disrupt hormone production, which can lead to an increase in appetite.

Children and adolescents who suffer from obesity are at a higher risk for various sleep disorders. Although researchers are still continuing to study this relationship, many believe this association involves metabolic and neuroendocrine/hormonal physiology and other factors. These sleep disorders can be categorized into four functional categories, including insufficient sleep quantity, poor sleep quality, inappropriate timing of the sleep period, and primary disorders of excessive daytime sleepiness.

Depression

It's totally normal for a child or teen to feel down or irritable from time to time, but if it's happening consistently there could be a deeper problem. Depression can occur early in life and cause serious consequences later in life. There are, of course, many different factors that can lead to depression or depressive symptoms.

Research has indicated that depression (in children and adults) is often linked to insomnia and other sleep problems. Depression and lack of quality sleep also share common symptoms, like fatigue, loss of interest, and depressed mood. Researchers have found that depression in children can be affected by the duration and quality of sleep they get each night.

It is rare to see depressive symptoms in youth before puberty, but the rates increase drastically in adolescence. Some argue that before puberty children's sleep is "protected" against disruptions. Young children are able to reach the deepest level of sleep, whereas adolescents often cannot. Many suffering from depression, including children and adults, report "sleep complaints" like having trouble falling asleep, having difficulty waking up, etc. These are considered subjective findings; there are also objective measures of research done through laboratory-based sleep studies that examine some of the physiological characteristics of sleep. Some studies have found that children with subjective sleep complaints do not always correlate with objective measures. This suggests a patient's perception of their sleep may differ from objective measures.

Clearly, quality sleep and these chronic diseases have a complex relationship. Many research reviews use the term bidirectional, functioning in two directions. Children and adolescents diagnosed with ADHD, Obesity, or Depression might experience sleep deficiency because of their diagnosis. It could also be the other way around, with sleep deficiency causing a misdiagnosis.

Please consult with a doctor if you have any concerns.

What you Can Do as a Teacher

Teachers can only do so much. If you suspect any students are struggling due to sleep deficiency you certainly can't go home with them and make them go to bed at a reasonable hour. But, you can do what you do best... educate!

Educate parents and students (depending on their age) about good sleep hygiene. Rip out the parent handout in the back of this issue on p. 103, fill in the blank (using the info on the sheet), and make copies to send home with students.

Sources:
>> CDC: Sleep in Middle and High School Students
>> PubMed.NCBI: Attention-deficit/hyperactivity Disorder With Obstructive Sleep Apnea: A Treatment Outcome Study
>> NCBI study: Sleep Disturbances in Pediatric Depression
>> Harvard.edu: Sleep Deprivation and Obesity
>> ScienceDaily: Children's Mental Health is Affected by Sleep Duration
>> CDC: Data and Statistics about ADHD
>> ClinMedJournals
>> PubMed.gov: Obstructive Sleep-Disordered Breathing in Children

HANDS IN THE EARTH

(No Garden Required!)

Sow the seeds of a lifelong love for nature by introducing your sprouts to these playful and rewarding projects with plants

Text: Mandy Allen/ Bureaux
Production: Jeanne Botes
Photographs: Warren Heath/ Bureaux

Kids will get a kick out of completing these tactile, all-season activities that merge imagination, creativity, botany and a little bit of practical magic. You also don't need acres of garden to dig in – if you have a sunny windowsill, you're good to go. With an emphasis on upcycling and sustainability, each of these easy projects is designed to encourage children to engage with nature, not tech. As well as the fun of getting their hands dirty, the bigger reward lies in watching something grow that they have nurtured themselves, thereby encouraging them to care for and appreciate all forms of life.

 ## BEAN THERE

Germinating beans with cotton wool, water and a bit of sunshine is a classic project for budding horticulturalists. It's an especially appealing activity for younger children thanks to how quickly the bean grows.

YOU WILL NEED:

>> Dried beans
(broad beans, sugar beans and butter beans will all work well)
>> Cotton wool
>> A glass container
>> A sunny windowsill

INSTRUCTIONS:

1. Place a layer of cotton wool in the bottom of a small Mason jar or other clear glass container such as an old jam or mustard jar.

2. Slip your dried beans in on the sides so that kids can have a clear view of the day-to-day changes.

3. Place another thin layer of cotton wool on top of the beans and gently press down.

4. Wet, but do not soak, the cotton wool.

5. Place on a sunny windowsill and wait for the magic to happen. The beans should start to germinate after about three days.

TIPS:

>> Water the cotton whenever it feels dry to the touch.
>> When the sprouts are around 8 inches tall they can be transferred, cotton wool included, to a planter or into the ground.
>> Beans love to climb: support them on a beanpole, trellis, or bamboo or wooden frames.

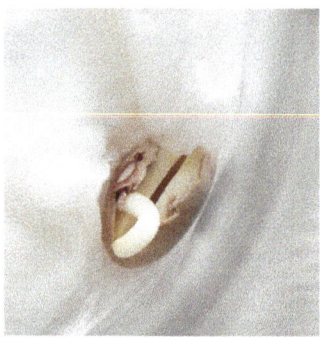   

2 STALKING ON EGGSHELLS

This cracking idea recycles egg shells, transforming them from kitchen refuse into nutrient rich eco-containers for growing flowers from seed.

YOU WILL NEED:

>> Cleaned and dry eggshell halves
>> Egg carton
>> Potting soil
>> Teaspoon
>> Spray-bottle filled with water
>> A long needle or pin
>> Flower seeds such as marigolds, cosmos, cornflowers, nasturtiums, pansies and sweet peas

INSTRUCTIONS:

1. Crack the eggs and pour the yolk and white into a bowl for cooking.

2. Rinse eggshell halves well, making sure to remove the fine membrane, and leave to dry.

3. Using a long needle, firmly but carefully poke a hole in the bottom of the shell from the inside. This is for drainage.

4. Lightly spray the eggshells with a fine mist of water.

5. Fill the shells about 3/4 of the way with potting soil using a teaspoon and level out with your fingers.

6. Gently press a few seeds into the soil using the instructions on the packet as a guide to suitable depth.

7. Place each egg container back into the carton.

8. Place in a sunny spot and wait for them to sprout.

9. Water with a spray bottle accordingly.

10. Once the seedlings are large enough, gently crack the eggshell containers and replant them into a pot or container in a place they will thrive.

11. Continue caring for the seedlings according to packet instructions until they bloom.

TIPS:
>> Once you've emptied the contents of the eggshell for use in cooking, rinse the shells and boil them up for a few minutes. This removes any remaining egg residue plus hardens the shells to prevent breakage. (Make sure you have poked your small drainage hole in the bottom of the shell before boiling.)
>> Remove any small bits of shell before potting with soil so that the opening is not too jagged.
>> Try broccoli, radish, carrot, and tomato seeds for homegrown veggies.

 # MAKING A SCENE

Inspired by the terrarium trend and museum dioramas, there's great fun to be had in planting up a clear container with succulents, moss and plastic wildlife.

YOU WILL NEED:

>> An assortment of glass or clear plastic/acrylic containers (terrariums, vases, Mason jars, or small fish bowls or tanks)
>> Child-friendly, spike-free succulents
>> Spray-bottle filled with water
>> Small pebbles as well as decorative stones
>> Potting soil
>> Moss (available from nurseries)
>> Plastic animal toys (or specific items for a biome or historical site to make this a dual learning experience for older students)

INSTRUCTIONS:

1. Place a generous layer of small stones or pebbles in the bottom of the container.

2. Top with soil, leaving a few inches of space at the top for plants (depending on their size) and small plastic toys.

3. Plant the succulents and create scenes using the toys and moss.

4. Spray with a fine mist of water as needed.

TIPS:

>> A terrarium makes a great DIY gift for little friends: pop a suitable container, several small succulents and a mini spray-bottle into a gift box along with soil, pebbles and plastic toys sorted into separate Ziploc bags. Don't forget hand-written instructions.
>> There's no limit to how creative you can get: think colorful gravel, fairies and toadstools, and dinosaurs.
>> Before assembling your terrarium, mark the inside of the jar with dots of glow-in-the-dark paint to up the cool factor.

YOU WILL NEED:
>> Plain white plastic pots
>> Succulents or indoor plants
>> Soil
>> Permanent markers

4 HAIR RAISING POTTED PERSONALITIES

Let kids decorate their own plastic pots with cute faces and then fill them with succulents and indoor plants to resemble funky hairstyles.

INSTRUCTIONS:

1. Give the kids their own pots and let them have free reign in drawing faces with permanent marker.

2. Help them fill the pots with soil and their chosen plants.

3. Leave the potted personalities indoors or on the balcony in a good spot and let students take care of the watering (and cutting back if necessary).

TIPS:

>> Avoid succulents with small thorns that can stick in little hands.
>> Herbs such as chives, parsley, rosemary, thyme and basil also make for funny-looking hairdos and can be sent home for parents as purposeful gifts. It sure beats a sticky, glue-y tissue paper craft!
>> Older children can use ceramic markers on terracotta pots to design pretty patterns or more elaborate drawings.

GROWTH SPURTS

Let children observe the magic of a how a cutting grows its roots – a quick way to propagate plants for free and a valuable lesson in caring for and appreciating just how awesome nature really is.

YOU WILL NEED:

>> A sterilized medium-sized glass bottle
>> Cuttings from healthy plants that will root easily without nursery-bought rooting hormones. Try species such as African violet, geranium, mint, wandering Jew, impatiens, or philodendron.

INSTRUCTIONS:

1. Help your students cut a three to six-inch section of stem from a healthy-looking plant by making a clean, angled snip above a leaf node.

2. Let them remove leaves from the bottom 1/3 or half of the cutting so you are left with a bare stalk and a few leaves on the top section.

3. Put the cutting in the bottle of water, submerging only the leafless stem.

4. Place the bottle in a place that gets partial sunlight and that is neither too hot nor too cold.

5. Once the roots are several inches long the cutting is ready to transplant into soil.

TIPS:

> Keep the water topped off and replace once a week or sooner if it becomes cloudy.
> Let the kids feel like mini scientists by displaying their cuttings in "vases" made of test tubes or beakers.
> Upcycled glass bottles filled with cuttings, displayed en masse from a metal frame, will create an eye-catching decorative element.

6. ROOTS & SHOOTS

Put your zero waste lifestyle aspirations into practice by showing kids that it's entirely possible – and super simple – to re-grow new organic vegetables from scraps.

YOU WILL NEED:

>> Small glass container, deep dish or a drinking glass / small pots
>> Soil
>> Garlic cloves / the thick base of a celery

INSTRUCTIONS:

To regrow celery:

1. Once you have used all the stalks on your bunch of celery, place the base in a container, deep dish or glass with clean, room-temperature water.

2. Leave it on the windowsill or somewhere that the base will get gentle sunlight.

3. New leaves should start to grow within five days.

4. Once the leaves are a little bigger, you can transfer your celery base into a pot filled with potting soil.

5. Plant the base in the soil with the leaf tips exposed and place in a spot that gets generous sunlight.

6. Water regularly.

7. After a week or two you should see stalks start to emerge.

To regrow garlic:

1. Try to buy organic garlic to begin with. This should ensure that it has not been chemically treated which often prevents sprouting.

2. Fill a pot with potting soil and plant cloves (sprouting or not) around one to two centimeters down so they are covered.

3. Leave on a sunny windowsill or spot on the balcony or in the garden.

4. Water regularly but do not soak the soil or the cloves will rot.

5. Your garlic sprouts should start to push through the soil after about a month.

6. After several months you should notice hard, grass-like leaves growing from the center of the plant.

7. Once these start to curl and brown, your garlic is ready to harvest.

TIPS:

>> In the initial stages of growing celery from the base, keep the water clear and fresh.
>> The process of regrowth can be repeated indefinitely for both vegetables.
>> Spring onions (also known as green onions) and chives can be regrown by cutting them about four inches from the base of the root and standing them in a glass of clean water on a sunny windowsill.

7
TRACKING TAGS

Kids can keep track of what they're growing (and you get to slip in a little spelling lesson along the way) by crafting cute washi tape flags and jotting down plant names onto them.

YOU WILL NEED:

>> Plain washi tape
>> Scissors
>> Markers
>> Wooden chopsticks or skewers

INSTRUCTIONS:

1. Cut a piece of washi tape to the length you'd like your flag to be.

2. Wrap that piece of washi in half around the top of the wooden stick.

3. Trim further if it's too long and cut a small triangle out of the centre to make a flag shape.

4. Write down the name of the herb or plant and stick the chopstick into the soil so that the flag sits above the top leaves.

TIPS:

>> If your students can't yet read, come up with a color code together that will help identify the different plants: orange for rosemary, pink for mint, yellow for tomatoes, green for lettuce, and so on.

>> Vary the shapes of the flags for interest.

 LET'S BE FRONDS

You say potato, I say beautiful indoor plant... The trailing, vine-like leaves of a sweet potato make for a whimsical and unusual addition to your collection of indoor plants. Kids will take pride in knowing that they have grown something so unusual and, quite frankly, cool.

YOU WILL NEED:

>> A few healthy, wrinkle-free sweet potatoes (even better if little sprouts are beginning to shoot out of the sweet potato 'eyes')

>> Clean glass jars and bottles with wide enough necks to place the potatoes into

INSTRUCTIONS:

1. Fill the jars almost to the top with water and place the bottom of the sweet potato into it so that it is resting in the water.

2. Keep at least the top 1/3 of the potato out of the water.

3. Place in a sunny or semi-sunny spot and wait for the magic to happen.

4. Vines with stems will begin to sprout in a few weeks.

TIPS:
>> Maintain the health of your sweet potato vines and the mother plant by keeping the water in your container clean. Change once a week or when it becomes murky.

>> Snip off any vines that have started to brown and wither.

OUR TOP PICKS FOR *extensions* TO INCREASE EFFICIENCY

EXTENSIONS

With extensions, you can tailor and customize your browser's behavior however you prefer.

Today's technology is nothing short of incredible. We have basically any information we want right at our fingertips, high-quality cameras wherever we go, and apps for every need. Oftentimes, we overlook an important aspect of technology: Google Chrome add-ons and extensions. Extensions help you customize your browser experience. These can be found right after your URL box. Add-ons are extra tools for Docs, Forms, Slides, and Sheets. Here are some awesome extensions and add-ons for anyone in the world of education.

LINER
With Liner, you can highlight the important text in various web articles. It automatically saves the articles and highlights to your account. It makes the organization super easy and consistent. When you go to make your bibliography, just go to your account and all of the links are saved for you!

SPRINT READER
A speed-reader extension is a huge time saver if you are doing a lot of research because it enables you to fly through the material. Keep in mind, if you teach ESL students or struggling learners, this extension may not be a good fit because students aren't exposed to a lot of language and it's very fast-paced.

SCREENCASTIFY
This awesome extension allows you to easily make video tutorials for your students that you can post for them to watch at their own pace. After installing the extension, click the icon and record your screen to show your students steps to take. They'll be able to see your cursor move on your screen.

INSERT LEARNING
This free extension is simply amazing, especially if you have students who get overwhelmed or bored with reading long articles. Essentially, IL enables you to turn any article on the internet into an interactive lesson. You simply read through the article, highlight, and click the tools in the sidebar to insert questions, discussion topics, sticky notes, and even videos! Your students' responses go straight to your dashboard.

GOOGLE READ&WRITE
This extension allows you to make websites and files on Google drive more accessible. It supports both reading and writing for different ability levels and learning styles. There are tools like text-to-speech to hear words, passages, or whole documents read aloud with easy-to-follow dual color highlighting or word prediction to offer suggestions for the current or next word as you type. Teachers can get a free premium subscription for this extension.

TABSCISSORS
This extension allows you to take two different tabs that you have open in your window and evenly split them, so you can see half of each tab on your screen at the same time. This can be really helpful if you're trying to enter grades on a separate page, or view one site as a reference while working in another.

TALK AND COMMENT
This extension allows you to record voice notes and paste the link to hear them wherever you want on the web. There are so many opportunities to make the most of this in the classroom. Use it in Google Classroom, Google Docs, Gmail, and more. Teachers find this handy when giving feedback or dictating personal notes.

DISCOVER chrome extensions

MINDMEISTER

Have your students interact with the content. This add-on will make a bulleted list into a mind map by using the first bullet point as the root, and then creating sub-topics that branch off. It's easy to use, imports directly into the google doc, and is visually appealing. Use this app for helping kids organize information.

EASYBIB

Essentially, this add-on creates a bibliography for you! When students are typing a paper in Google Docs, they can open this EasyBib add-on. (It will come up on the right-hand side.) Then, students enter the website URL, book ISBN or Title, etc, and it automatically formats, alphabetizes, generates, and inserts your bibliography straight into the paper. Even if you don't choose to use tools like this, be aware that students might be.

FLIPPITY

Flippity is a series of templates you can use in Sheets. With Flippity, you can quickly and easily create flashcards with images and videos, quiz games, crossword puzzles, bingo games, spinners, progress trackers, and much more. You fill in the template provided with your content, go to "file," and select "publish to the web." Then go back to Add-ons, and select "Flippity.net." Click the link, and you will be directed to your interactive activity!

AUTOMASTERY

This add-on enables you to effortlessly differentiate the students' learning by giving them a diagnostic quiz and sorting everyone into three groups- beginning, intermediate, and mastery. (You set these scores.) Then it sends them an email with continued assignments you've set up that are appropriate to their level, based on their scores. Visit leahcleary.com for an in-depth post detailing exactly how to use AutoMastery.

ADD-ONS

Add-ons allow you to customize any application within Google Drive (Google Docs, Sheets, Forms, and Slides). To find them in Docs, Sheets, and Slides just click "Add-ons" in the toolbar. When using Forms, click "More" in the toolbar.

ORANGESLICE TEACHER RUBRIC

This tool, created specifically for teachers, makes creating rubrics efficient. It transforms a holistic rubric into a percentage or points grade and inserts it within a student's document. The teacher can select various preset or customizable categories, grade it, and give instant feedback to the student.

OUR TOP PICKS FOR add-ons THAT WILL MAKE YOUR TEACHING DAY GO MORE SMOOTHLY

BY KELLY BARENDT
WITH ED. TECH EXPERT
LEAH CLEARY

leahcleary.com

CLASSROOM TOUR

Mrs. Craven's Kindergarten classroom comes to life with a farmhouse-style pretend center, beautiful greenery, and a variety of peaceful, uncluttered zones for kinders to read and learn. "Our farmhouse play kitchen allows students to work on social skills and problem solving," Marie Craven, a 10 year teaching veteran explains.

"This is our reading center where the students love to sit on the sofa and the tree stump cushions to read." (below)

The students are able to find sight words by using the portable word wall frames that are placed on all tables. These portable word walls are housed in Ikea frames for students to easily flip through and reference during writing station work.

MARIE CRAVEN
@teachingwithmrscraven

"My students are the absolute best! They come to class every day eager to learn with their minds and hearts open for everything this teacher has to offer. I teach the most rewarding grade... Kindergarten.

They are like little sponges, ready to soak in all the knowledge that is given to them. It is incredible to see the growth they show in academics, and also socially.

A lot of the items in my classroom you can find on Amazon. (I can't live without Amazon Prime!) Other things I made by hand or found on sale at Ross or in the Target Bulls Eye Area. The cubby containers came from an amazing store... Dollar Tree!

My students love the book center! They love to sit on the sofa and tree stump cushions and read. Other favorites are all the different kinds of seating that I offer in my room. We have stools, chairs with arms, floor cushions, wobble stools, etc."

balancing work and life

When asked how she balances teaching obligations with everything else in her life, Marie confidently explains, "I have had to learn this over the years. I remember when I first started I would spend so many long nights at the school every day, even weekends. I would even come home and spend more time working on school work. After I had my son, I realized that my students and my son aren't going to get the best of me if I don't take care of myself or if I prioritize my work over my personal life. I am NOT the last car in the parking lot anymore and I am still as amazing a teacher as I was or better than when I would stay way too late."

the right rug

Marie shares, "I love how cozy it feels in the classroom. One of my favorite pieces is the new rug for whole group meetings."

positivity

"I strive to have a positive learning environment that is inviting and cozy. I want the students to enter my classroom and know that they are loved and safe. I want my students to know that I care about them and want only the best for them. I love to promote positive peer relationships by working in small groups or partners on tasks throughout the day. I love to see students problem solving together and learning how to be kind to one another," Marie explains.

D.I.Y. upgrades

Marie painted old wooden cabinets white and added a marble-look contact paper to create a beautiful countertop and backsplash around her classroom sink area.

repurposing

Storing chrome books and iPads in a dish rack keeps them from bumping together, and each student can access the right one as needed. It's a cheap and simple solution that keeps cords all pointing the same way.

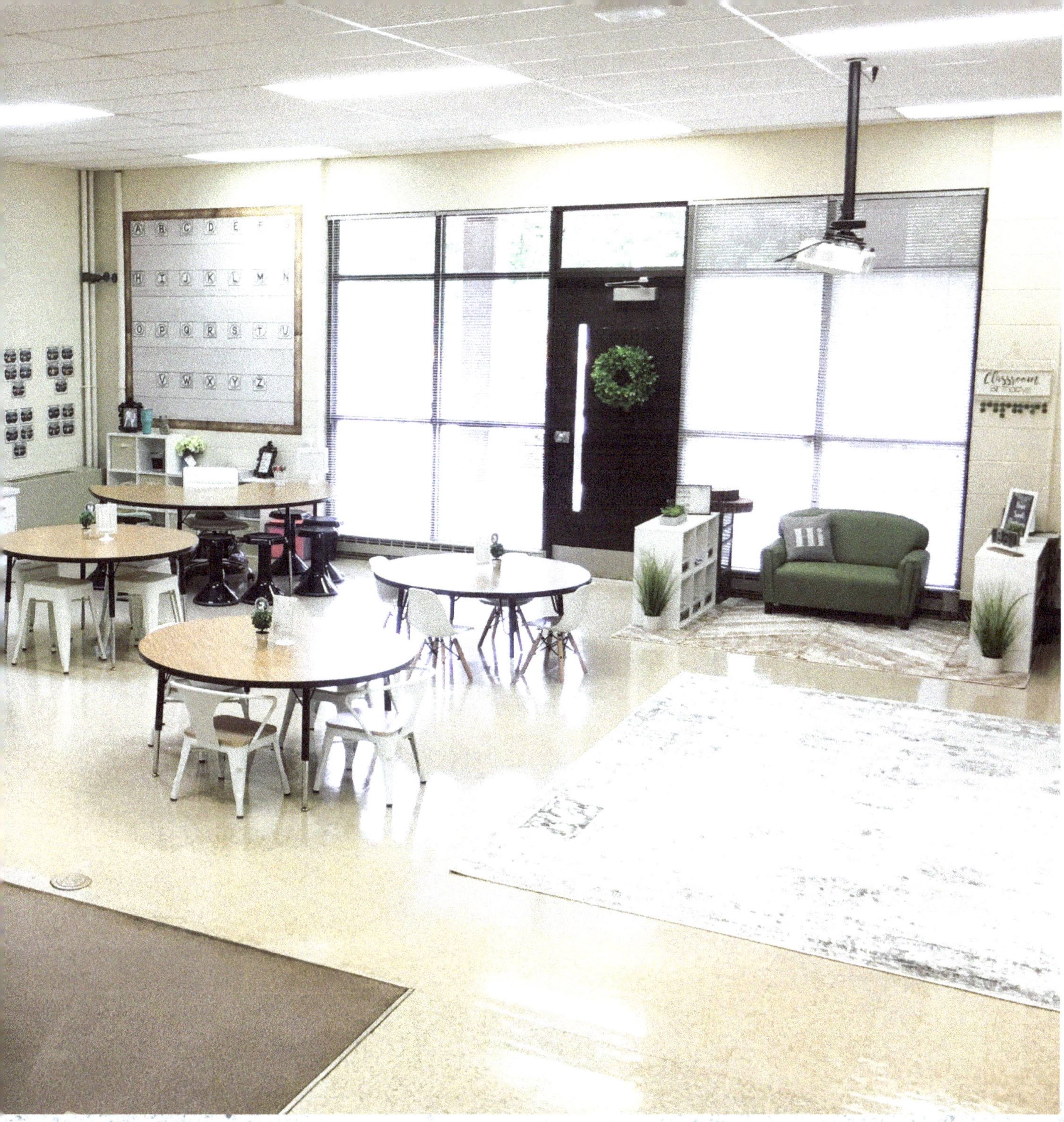
Hi

welcome
to our
beautiful
chaos

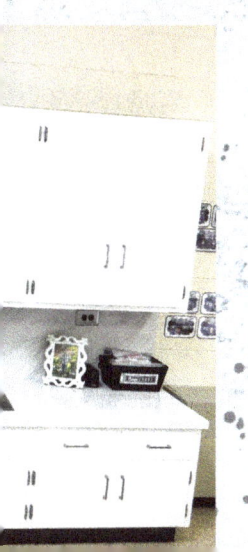

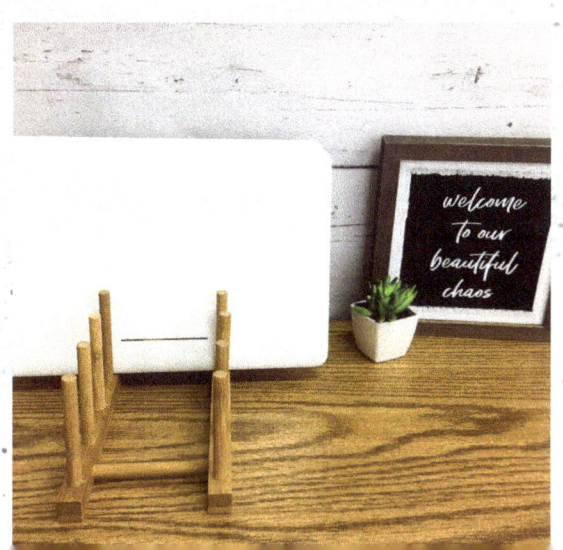

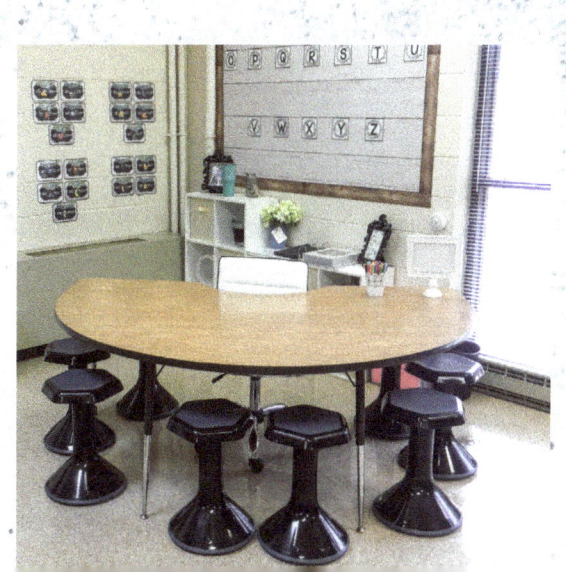

cozy atmosphere

Marie enjoys the warm feeling that her classroom offers, saying "I love how cozy and homey it feels in my room. I love how inviting it is to visitors but also how organized the classroom is."

Magnetic wooden caddies stick to the whiteboard and come in handy for keeping markers organized and close at hand.

gratitude

Reflecting on her teaching career, Marie shares, "I am grateful for my administrator at my school. We are blessed to have such a caring and supportive leader. She wants what is best for the students and backs us up 100%. I wouldn't be able to do the things I feel would benefit my students without her supporting our decisions."

station organization

"This basket cart has been the best for organizing different stations," Marie explains. "The baskets hold literacy centers, math centers, engineering, and block center materials. The students know exactly where to find each station."

BEHIND THE LOTUS PROJECT

supporting teen girls in finding their own

POWER
FREEDOM
BEAUTY
COURAGE
VALUE

"I was watching too many girls with tons of potential feeling 'stuck.' Stuck with the idea that they weren't ever good enough or the idea that 'this is just the way it is.' They were believing the lies that we're told about our bodies, our emotions and our femininity. At the time, I had only uncovered my truth about my value and I couldn't have them wait until they were 33 to start recognizing theirs. I had to start teaching them.

AND THE LOTUS PROJECT WAS BORN."

by LaRissa Paras, Founder of the Lotus Project and LP Inspire
@thelotusproject

are whole
feel empowered
gain confidence
feel a sense of belonging
be themselves & unapologetic
true to wants & needs
feel heard
feel like their voices matter
feel strong
feel connected
share what they learn to empower each other
compete less & build community more
brave. To make progress & not expect perfection
stop negative self talk, promote a positive inner dialog

WHEN

before → break the mold   NOW. → to stop the next body trend

grow bloom

"the set-up"   Society's judgements   stigma

constructs

make you feel small   oppressed voices

during a time when we are feeling small   before media

during a time unspoken issues expectations

invisible mold

We've been told and keep telling our girls that "you can have it all" and while this is true, we also have to emphasize that we can't "have it all" ALL AT ONCE. It's too much pressure. Somewhere along the line the idea of "having it all" translated into "you HAVE to do it all." This is an overwhelming and unfair expectation to have. We need to learn and to teach people to tap into their inner instincts and use their voices to express their wants and needs and to set healthy boundaries in our personal and professional lives.

Not just for young women, but for many young people... the shame of raising your hand and speaking up can be very scary. Make your classroom a safe space, encourage the process of learning as opposed to the perfect answer. Build relationships and show your mistakes and humanity to them. Be vulnerable in front of them. If they know that mistakes equal progress, and that there's nothing to be ashamed about, you're going to get more brave participation. More learning will take place.

2020 ushered in my 20th year of teaching! I've taught in New York and Michigan, my home state. I teach World History and Current Issues in Greenville, where I have been now for almost 15 years. I have co-authored two books, published the Lotus Project Curriculum solo, and run my own Lotus Project in my building while trying to get it into the hands of other educators. I'm a cognitive coach and I'm working on a new book. I'm also married and we are raising two young men, who are great humans! I am a total Francophile and love all things French... cheese, bread, stripes, wine, architecture, history, people, and pastries. Our June 2020 trip was cancelled and I'm just waiting for the green light to start planning again.

The Lotus Project is a mentorship program to encourage young women to strengthen their inner selves in order to reach their full potential and to recognize their value and beauty. The Lotus Project is built on the principles of sisterhood, inner strength, confidence, health, relationships, gratitude, and responsibility. The curriculum (that is for sale) is made up of activities, conversation starters, creative ways to connect, and journaling prompts.

Photography by Anna Ellerbroek

In the process of developing this program to instill self-confidence in female students, LaRissa narrowed in on eight key concepts that she shares on the next page. These will help you guide your own teen girls toward self-actualization.

HELP YOUR OWN YOUNG WOMEN UNEARTH THEIR POWER, FREEDOM, BEAUTY, COURAGE, AND VALUE

with the 8 Pillars that LaRissa Teaches her Lotus Project Students:

AN ACTION PLAN

SISTERHOOD

Show your young women that they have more in common than they realize.

Here's how this pillar looks in the Lotus Project Program:

During your first meeting, establish the tone for your sessions. The young women will work through getting-to-know-you activities while establishing group norms and creating declarations to themselves. This session will also introduce the girls to the journaling component that is a part of every session.

INNER BEAUTY

Ask them to describe someone in their life that they admire and tell why. Remind them that these traits aren't about outside appearances but about their actions and heart.

Here's how this pillar looks in the Lotus Project Program:

This second session opens our eyes to how they interpret beauty, strength and confidence. They will do some inner reflection while you lead them through "The Most Important Person" activity. You'll introduce them to the idea of self-care and more journaling.

A HEALTHY YOU

Be vulnerable with your own story about your health journey so that they know that they're not alone.

Here's how this pillar looks in the Lotus Project Program:

In the Lotus Project we focus on the WHOLE PERSON, not just the physical healthiness of a person. You'll get the girls to start thinking of these five areas: Self Reflection, Fitness, Food, Sleep, and Spirit. You'll emphasize that health is a lifelong journey and that it's not just about looks, but about mental health as well.

GRATITUDE

Keep a log of things you appreciate and are grateful for. Even start your class with this as a warm up.

Here's how this pillar looks in the Lotus Project Program:

We can't always control our circumstances, but we can control our attitude and our reactions. In this session we'll start with appreciating some of the people in our life, starting with our own Lotus circle. We then use the power of a sticky note to spread some cheer in our building... on lockers, classrooms, office desks, janitorial closets, etc. You will teach your girls what it means to be a #LoveNinja. This session also gives a lot of ideas for giving back to the community through different acts of service.

MEDIA

Remind kids that companies and influencers are selling something and trying to make you feel like you're "not enough" in order to sell their products. Work on your inner guide and know your "why" for what you allow your mind to ingest.

Here's how this pillar looks in the Lotus Project Program:

It is so vital for all of us to evaluate how our screens are affecting our psyche. In this session you will talk about the "comparison monster," what it means to be a good human, the stereotype boxes men and women find themselves in, and all of the editing and photoshopping that goes into advertisement and other images. You'll watch a video about being brave vs. being perfect. This session is a deep and curious one.

RELATIONSHIPS

Teach boundaries! Setting boundaries around our wants and needs (and sticking to them) tells the world that we love and respect ourselves... and expect the same respect out of our relationships.

Here's how this pillar looks in the Lotus Project Program:

Relationships are not just romantic. Explore all the ways for relationships to be healthy and unhealthy. Start with a communication team building activity and move into some thoughtful explorations about what we see around us. "Rings of trust" define true friend vs. acquaintance. Watch a video on relational aggression, which is especially affecting our girls. Finally, you will go through 8 role play scenarios to build confidence and to sort through the "what can I do?" thoughts.

LOOKING AHEAD

Setting goals is a multi-step process. Start with the end goal first and then back-track to break it down into smaller parts.

Here's how this pillar looks in the Lotus Project Program:

Teach the girls the craft of setting goals in a strategic way that doesn't seem overwhelming. By looking at goal setting "backwards by design" we start with long term, mid term and short term goals. The short term is more like your daily to-do list. By breaking things into chunks we can see the whole picture. Talk about the importance of having an aspirational goal - something you'll always work toward.

MY FUTURE SELF

Help your kids to brainstorm about where they want to be in the future and be sure to get them to dream big! This is such a fun and hopeful thing to bring to the table.

Here's how this pillar looks in the Lotus Project Program:

In our final session you will craft a book of letters to your future selves. Each letter has a different theme, focusing on promises, dreams, things to try, things to remember, pep talks, etc. Looking ahead and being our own cheerleaders is vital to our growth as humans.

Use these eight pillars to structure your sessions as you help your own teens uncover their beauty, confidence, and inherent value. For more guidance, access an already prepared full curriculum of these eight sessions at thelotusproject.net

SNAILS + FAIRYDUST
MIND OF A MAKER

Darcy Le Fleming
@snailsandfairydust

I find that the slow and deliberate act of beading can feel like a meditation or a prayer and even when I have set aside my beading for extended periods of time, I always find myself returning to this art form during the most challenging times in my life.

I am the mother of two magical little girls ages 10 and 4. The name Snails and Fairydust is inspired by the way they view the world around them and how they can find wonder and joy in the things that adults take for granted, like watching snails leave a slime trail or building a fairy house out of foraged materials.

A bowl of rainbow seed beads in the art cabin of my Girl Scout camp got me interested in the craft of beading when I was twelve. I still remember the excitement of stringing those beads onto fishing line to make friendship bracelets and the smell of the cabin. I came home from camp begging for more beads, so my mother bought me a beading loom.

Since then, it has always been something that I return to. I love the idea of creating rituals in our lives and I hope that the pieces I make spark the creation of rituals for the person who purchases it.

I think most people are completely mystified by beading and think they could never do it, but it is so much easier than people realize. I have been working on tutorials to make the art of beading more accessible. I want everyone to learn to bead. I think it is so good for slowing down and perfect for people who find traditional meditation difficult.

I love the idea of creating rituals in our lives and I hope that the pieces I make spark the creation of rituals for the person who purchases it.

I want everyone to learn to bead. I think it is so good for slowing down and perfect for people who find traditional meditation difficult.

CREATIVE INSPIRATION FROM DARCY

Tell us about your creative workspace.

My workspace is an old wardrobe that I turned into a workspace with a desk that drops down when you open the doors. It is perfect because I can close the doors when I am done and not have to worry about cleaning up.

How do you balance work and life?

I'm not sure anyone has the answer to this.

What are you most grateful for?

I am grateful to have a supportive husband who is also an amazing father. I could not be the parent or artist I want to be without him.

How do you get inspired for the next piece? Does your work or style transition over time?

I am inspired by nature and color combinations that speak to me. I used to create pieces based on what I thought was fashionable at the time, but now I create things that I love.

What is your favorite book?

The Artist's Way by Julia Cameron

What do you listen to while you work?

My current Spotify stations are Marvin Gaye Radio, Women of Folk, Norah Jones Radio and All Out 80's.

What strategies help you carve out time to create?

If I am in a creative dry spell, I like to give myself small goals without expecting myself to "produce" anything. For instance, I will say, "This week I will just play around with beading for 45 minutes a day."

Try to carve out small dedicated times to create and dedicate a space where your supplies are ready for you to just get started so you are not wasting time setting up and putting things away.

Also, if you have children, find a craft you can do together so you are getting your parenting and creative time in at the same time. I like to give my girls beading projects appropriate for their ages. The three of us sit together and work on our own projects.

What fills your soul?

Being a mother.

Share your favorite mom hack.

I made a huge list of activities for my daughters to do when they are bored. It has been really helpful during the pandemic to just refer to that list when I am ready to just throw them in front of a screen.

How does your environment impact you? And what do you do to ensure your workspace and home space are nurturing?

I like to keep a lot of plants in our home and my daughters are always bringing home rocks, sticks, and plants, so I like to keep surfaces clear for them to place their collections.

Living in Brooklyn, I find it is important to me to keep a connection to nature as much as possible.

I'm Virginia, a kindergarten teacher at St. Mary Catholic School in Berea, Ohio. This is my 12th year at St. Mary's and my 15th year of teaching overall. I took a break from teaching (for 22 years) to be at home while our 8 children were young. I have been married to my husband, Mark, for 36 years, and now that he is retired he comes in to help in my classroom and has even been able to sub for me on a few occasions! I have mentored many students, both during their methods courses and during student teaching. I really enjoy seeing them grow in confidence as the semester progresses, and I try to fade into the background so that it feels like their classroom by the last few weeks.

I'm Kelly. I studied Early Childhood Education in undergrad and then earned my Masters in Education specializing in Early Childhood from The Ohio State University. Due to health concerns, I decided being a classroom teacher wouldn't be the right fit, but I am so fortunate to be able to use my background in Education in a different way that works for me. I had student teaching experiences in both 3rd grade and 1st grade, where I learned to truly appreciate some of the words and actions of my mentors.

How to be a Good Mentor Teacher

Advice from both Sides : a Seasoned Mentor Teacher and a Former Student Teacher Compare Tips

If the next step in your teacher journey is becoming a mentor teacher, here are some insights to keep in mind.

MENTOR TEACHER

ADVICE FROM A MENTOR TEACHER:
Communication is key!
I start by establishing a relationship with my student teacher. It is important to be welcoming and encouraging. I make sure the student teacher understands what I expect from them and we schedule times during the week to have discussions. I try to make sure I praise what they do well in addition to offering tips for improvement in their lessons, demeanor and classroom management. I also communicate with their college supervisor and share both successes and concerns with the college supervisor. They usually have really good insight and can be very helpful if there are any areas of concern.

The Start (Week 1)
I have them start slowly. During the first week, I have them observe my teaching and classroom management. I model what I want to see in their lessons. For example:
>> I use "I can" statements so the students know what they will be learning.
>> I plan a good introduction to the lesson- something to grab students' attention.
>> I give clear instructions and explanations and try to explain new concepts in more than one way.
>> Most lessons include class practice of new skills as well as time for individual practice with intervention as needed.
>> I try to make a lot of positive comments to students regarding their questions, answers, behavior, insights, etc.

While I am teaching, I encourage the student teacher to circulate around the room and monitor and assist the students as they work. I also encourage the student teacher to make positive comments to students starting the first day and to establish a good rapport with the students. I like to discuss what they see in my instruction and classroom management and the philosophy behind it.

Planning (Week 2 onwards)
The student teacher starts planning and instructing for one subject for the first week, then we add one subject per week. We discuss the lesson together and what it might look like, then they plan it on their own but I am available for questions or suggestions.

I think it is important to realize that your student teacher is not you, and it is okay if they do things differently than you would, as long as the students are being treated properly and are learning the content. I review the lesson plan prior to their teaching it and give input to help build a successful lesson.

Teaching
During their lessons, I take notes and we discuss them afterward. I try to note both the strengths and weaknesses in the lessons. I note how they handled classroom management, I note if the learning objectives were met, and I note how the lesson was assessed.

When we discuss the lesson, I try to praise the positives and offer insight and strategies for improvement (if necessary). I like to ask the student-teacher how they think the lesson went and what they learned or took away from the lesson. I think it is important to let them make mistakes. They are not going to be perfect and this is part of the learning process. I find that they learn a lot from their mistakes and being able to "salvage" a not so great lesson is part of the teaching process (we have all been there!).

STUDENT TEACHER

MENTORING TIPS FROM A STUDENT TEACHER:

1. Make your student-teacher feel welcome. I was extremely nervous to meet my mentor teacher for the coming semester, but before school began, she invited me on a coffee date to meet and get to know each other. At Starbucks, she gave me a gift- a t-shirt with the school's mascot on it. You certainly don't have to give your ST a gift or go out on a coffee date, but her thoughtfulness meant so much to me. I felt welcomed into her classroom and like a member of the school community.

2. Sit down and lesson plan with your student-teacher. Show them your thought process on planning upcoming lessons. It's likely your ST has never done this in a school setting before, and it really helps to see how you go about it.

3. Gradually give more and more responsibility. At the beginning of the school year, I sat and observed my mentor teacher teaching reading groups. Eventually, she let me plan and instruct a few reading group lessons. By the end of the semester, I had my own reading group.

4. Think Out Loud. Similar to showing them how you plan, when you're thinking through a problem, explain your thought process. "Ava has been having a really hard time sitting still on the carpet. I'm going to ask her if she would prefer to pull up a chair to the back of the carpet," or, "I'd really like to see Cole concentrate better during Writing Workshop. Let's try giving him a differently lined paper, so he has more space for his words."

5. Model how to be a collaborative team member. In my first-grade student-teaching experience, the 4 first grade teachers made an awesome team; it was great to see how working together can greatly improve everything from behavior management to grading assessments. Be supportive, positive, and encouraging with your team members.

Immunity Support
COCKTAIL

Citrus fruits contain plenty of Vitamin C, which greatly improves the health of your immune system. It strengthens your body's natural barrier against pathogens.

Ginger has anti-bacterial and anti-inflammatory properties. It can even help activate the immune system against cancers!

This cocktail is delicious while offering a much needed immune boost for teachers.

Ingredients:
> 1 red grapefruit
> 1 lemon
> 1.5 oz. gin
> 0.5 oz. orange liqueur
> tonic water
> 1 tbsp. fine sugar
> 2 sprigs of mint leaves
> 1 slice of ginger root

Muddle the sugar, 6 mint leaves, and 1/2 oz. of lemon juice (juice from about 1/2 of a lemon) together until the sugar has ground the leaves well.

Put the muddled blend into a cocktail shaker.

Add 1/4 cup grapefruit juice (juice from about 1/2 of a grapefruit), the gin, the orange liqueur, and a pinch of grated ginger.

Shake with ice. Pour into a glass and top off with tonic.

Express the oil of a grapefruit peel by squeezing a slice of peel over the glass, then dropping it in. Garnish with a sprig of mint. Enjoy!

BURNOUT...
TEACHERS NEED REST

We all know someone who has left the profession or has seriously thought about leaving. Maybe you've considered it yourself. It's not uncommon. Teaching is not an easy job, and often leads to burnout.

We decided to dive into the statistics on teacher turnover, and ask questions like: Why do teachers leave? What are the trends over time? Where do teachers go? Do most teachers quit early in their careers or after a good amount of experience? How does the United States compare to other countries? Why does this matter? What can we do?

What are the stats?
>> Approximately 8% of teachers leave teaching every year and another 8% move to a different teaching job. (The U.S. teacher attrition rate was only 5 percent in the 1990s, so it's growing.)

>> Less than 1/3 of teacher attrition is due to retirement. (Many teachers are leaving in the beginning and the middle of their careers).

>> 30 percent of college graduates who became teachers were not in the profession five years later.

>> Well-regarded school systems in places like Canada, Finland, and Singapore have attrition rates closer to 3% or 4%, according to the report.

>> Teacher education enrollment dropped from 691,000 to 451,000, a 35 percent reduction, between 2009 and 2014.

>> Underprepared teachers are 2 to 3 times more likely to leave teaching than fully prepared teachers.

>> 31 states reported at least 82,000 positions filled by underqualified teachers, in addition to at least 5,000 unfilled vacancies during the school year.

>> Total turnover rates are highest in the South (16.7%) and lowest in the Northeast (10.3%), where states tend to offer higher pay, support smaller class sizes, and make greater investments in education.

Why do teachers leave?
Many sources state a consensus that poor working conditions play an essential role in teacher turnover. This can be narrowed down to poor compensation and a serious lack of resources. We can also attribute the problem to an increase in high-stakes testing. Many studies also found that a supportive principal is key to a positive experience as a teacher. Research suggests that principals who spend more time doing observations and giving feedback or coaching teachers often see greater achievement.

What are the trends?
Studies have shown that educators who specialize in math, science, special education, English language development, or foreign languages are more likely to leave their job. We see teacher shortages in these subjects all across the country.

Research has also shown that a teacher's path to certification plays a big role in how long they stay in the field. Teachers who went through an alternative certification program might have less of an attachment to teaching. 23% of teachers who were traditionally prepared left teaching by the end of their third year, but 45% of alternatively certified teachers left by the end of their third year.

Where do teachers go?
Teachers in high-poverty schools tend to move to more affluent districts or schools. The other way around is very rare. If teachers leave the profession before retirement, research shows that teachers tend to move to jobs that require similar skills, like healthcare or social workers. Many teachers are also drawn to administrative jobs, as opposed to teaching.

Why is this such a problem?
Teacher turnover is a problem for multiple reasons. First, it disrupts learning for students when teachers leave midyear. It also hurts parent-teacher relationships. Turnover also creates staffing issues for schools. There is a serious need for teachers in schools across the nation, and teacher turnover just exacerbates this. Teacher turnover rates also impact the school environment and can make it difficult to build a school community, which affects student learning.

Finally, high teacher turnover overwhelmingly hurts high-poverty schools the most, which serve mostly students of color. Generally, teachers who leave high-poverty schools tend to transfer to wealthier school districts, leaving a dire need for experienced teachers in high-poverty schools. These schools also have more alternatively certified teachers, who not only have a higher turnover rate but are also potentially less effective than highly-qualified teachers

What can we do about it?
As a teacher, you can improve teacher turnover by helping to create a supportive and collaborative school environment. If you've ever taught, you know the incredible demands on teachers. You know from day one, teachers have to figure out classroom management, lesson planning, professional development, parent communication, grading, differentiation, and, of course, actually teaching. Studies have shown that this has actually improved over the years; many new teachers are assigned a mentor. However, the ever-growing demands on teachers are not helping.

Teacher turnover rates in the U.S. reflect systemic challenges, and thus, require systemic change. Policymakers and practitioners have the power to improve working conditions that we already know would improve teacher turnover.

Stats from Economic Policy Institute

TEACHER TURNOVER

8% of teachers leave the profession every year, and another 8% moves to a different school

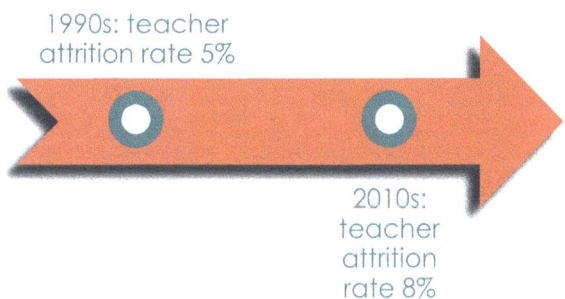

1990s: teacher attrition rate 5%

2010s: teacher attrition rate 8%

More than two-thirds of teachers leave before retirement

About one-third of college graduates who became teachers left the profession within 5 years

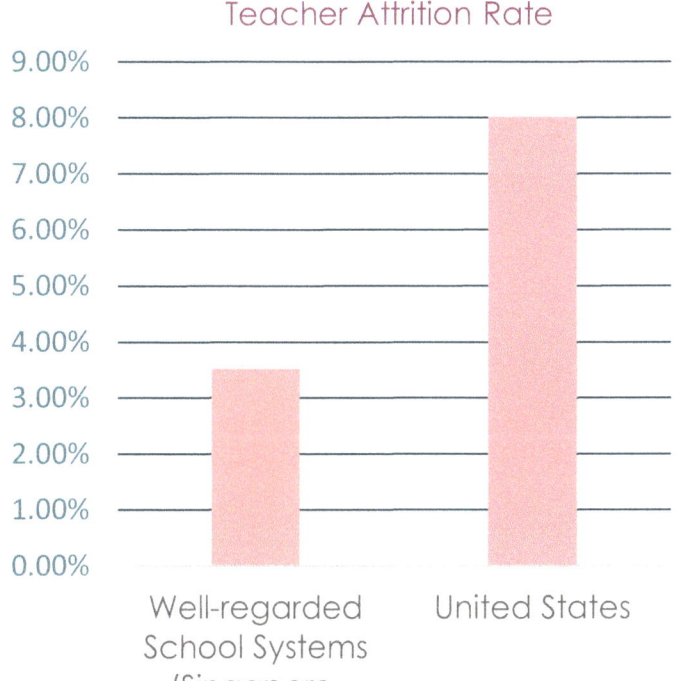

Teacher Attrition Rate

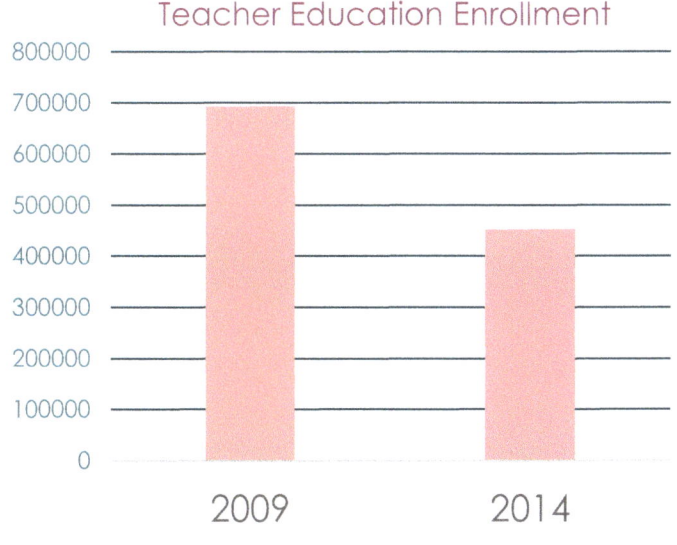

Teacher Education Enrollment

PASSING NOTES

Relationships are the foundation of leadership.
>> John C. Maxwell

What do you wish your administration would do differently?

I wish admin would TRUST teachers. When we ask for something, whether it be time, materials, policy, etc. it's because we are smart, experienced people "in the trenches" who see a need and know we could do a better job if granted the respectful space of hands off, non-micromanaging trust.

>> *Carolyn, 9-12 Family and Consumer Sciences*

Get input from teachers before making wholescale procedure or policy changes.

>> *Alice, 8th Grade Math*

It would help me (and the kids) a lot if our principal circulated around the school more often in a positive way. A pleasant drop in here and there without any stress attached to it would go a long way. I know he has a really full schedule, but even once a month for 2 minutes per room would do it.

>> *Anonymous*

I would like to see administrations trusting the professionals they hired. Too often, there seems to be micro-managing, second guessing, and playing sides. Simply trust the people you hired to do the best job they know how to do.

>> *Brittany, 6th Grade*

Honestly, I sometimes wish they'd be LESS flexible. Consistency is really important for school culture. When just one teacher is allowing shenanigans, or a single room is completely lacking in discipline, it transfers throughout the building to every single teacher as those kids flow from one class period to the next. Certain things are really hard to address on a teacher-to-teacher level, but impact everyone. If admin does not step up, students are frustrated, parents are frustrated, and teachers are frustrated.

>> *Anonymous*

boost your bath

Recipes for Making your Next Bath Do Double Duty as both Health and Comfort

MUSCLES AND JOINTS

To ease the ache of sore muscles and relieve tension, start with 2 cups of epsom salt. The magnesium in it is easily absorbed by the skin and helps reduce lactic acid buildup. Blend a tablespoon of coconut oil to act as an anti-inflammatory agent with 5 drops of sweet marjoram oil to reduce muscle stiffness and decrease spasms and pains. Add a scoop of shredded ginger, an anti-arthritic. For additional help with inflammation and circulation, add 2-3 drops of rosemary oil to the coconut oil before putting it into the bath.

HORMONE SUPPORT

If you suffer from PMS, a hot bath alone can help, but to enhance the effect of your soak, pour in a cup of Dead Sea salt, which is packed with minerals with healing properties. Add a tablespoon of coconut oil blended with a few drops of clary sage oil and a bit of neroli. Last, sprinkle in some rose petals. The clary sage oil helps to balance hormones and reduce cramping while the oil from the rose petals reduces pain and revitalizes skin. (Tip: Instead of gathering up the petals after, try a DIY "tea bag" or sachet.)

Do your research on the safety of different essential oils, salts, and other ingredients and consult a doctor if you have any questions relative to your specific health needs.

MIGRAINES OR SINUSES

If you struggle during allergy season, or have frequent migraines, a bath can offer relief. Blend 5 drops of peppermint essential oil, 3-5 drops of tea tree oil, and a few drops of eucalyptus or chamomile oil with a tablespoon of carrier oil, like coconut oil or jojoba oil. Once the essential oils are diluted in the carrier oil and mixed well, then add it to the warm bath and get in. Never add peppermint directly to the tub, or it can burn your skin.

DETOX

After a flight, or any other time you feel the need for a good detoxifying bath, try adding some bentonite clay. Use up to 1 cup per bath. Break the clay into small clumps and add it to hot running bath water. Add a few spoonfuls of baking soda and a cup of apple cider vinegar. For even more detoxifying power and a fresh scent, blend a few drops of lemon or grapefruit oil with a tablespoon of coconut oil and add that to the bathtub as well.

RELAXATION

When you need a break from stress and tension, start your bath with 2 cups of Himalayan pink salt. It's loaded with minerals including potassium, magnesium, copper, iron, and calcium. Blend a tablespoon of jojoba oil with 5 drops of lavender oil and a few drops of patchouli. The lavender is calming, and patchouli reduces depression and anxiety. If you do this bath at bedtime, add a bit of chamomile as well.

SKIN

To keep your skin healthy and glowing, draw up a lukewarm bath. While the water is still running, sprinkle in a cup of dry oatmeal, 1/2 cup of aloe vera gel, and 1/2 cup of coconut oil. Add a few pinches of calendula flowers. Calendula is soothing for skin and helps to heal any dryness or blemishes. (Tip: To avoid mess and keep your drain clear, place the calendula petals in a sachet or small bag.)

IMMUNITY

Teachers need extra strong immune systems. During flu and cold seasons, in addition to your epsom salts, add an immune blend to your bath. Combine a tablespoon of coconut oil with 3 drops of frankincense oil, 3 drops of clove oil, and 2 drops of oregano oil. Last, add 3 spoonfuls of shredded or ground ginger root.

5 Ways to Style a JUMPSUIT

CARMEN MYER @THEGOODCARMABLOG

One of my goals for 2020 has been to shop less and repurpose more of my old clothing. I didn't know how easy this would be since school was closed from March-September and I stayed at home for the majority of that time. I found myself going from doing online lesson planning on my sofa to Zoom meetings with coworkers and friends. I wanted to look presentable for the digital meetings but comfortable while being at home. I relied on the variety of jumpsuits I had to do just that! I could throw a sweatshirt over them while working and then exchange that sweatshirt for a cute pair of earrings and a cardigan for Zoom calls. I wanted to wear the most versatile item in my closet and I kept coming back to my jumpsuits each day. Here are a few of my favorite ways I chose to wear them.

Make your fit monochromatic

Add camo! This is a two-in-one style tip. Just like denim, I like adding a bit of camo to outfits to spice them up a bit. I'm still inspired by Destiny's Child's "Survivor" video when they made camo fashionable. Anyway, I also made this more of a monochromatic look by playing up all of the olive green I was wearing by adding a sage green headband.

Put on your favorite cardigan

Nothing beats a great cardigan. I feel like this looks like a completely different outfit while adding a touch of sweetness to the look. As a teacher, whenever I wear a cardigan I immediately think of Ms. Honey from the movie "Matilda" and try to channel her patience.

With a pop of leopard + belt it

This was my go to look for a quick walk around the block when I needed some fresh air and was going stir crazy!

4 This is what I would put on for a socially distanced front porch chat with friends. I just rolled up the pant legs and pinned them underneath the skirt. No one could even tell there were pants attached to that top and it transformed the entire look!

Get fancy with a skirt!

"Anyone can get dressed up and glamorous, but it is how people dress in their days off that are the most intriguing." >> Alexander Wang

Don't forget about denim

5 When in doubt, go with denim. It adds a touch of style to any outfit. Another great option would be tying the ends of a denim button down shirt over the top of your jumpsuit or around your waist. I hope you enjoy these looks and that this encourages you to play around with the items you already have in your closet!

DON'T MISS THE NEXT ISSUE

Get notifications from SnowDay Magazine by registering for our emails at snowdaymagazine.com

BONUS

We will send you our free minimag too!

P.S.

Come follow us on Instagram in the meantime! @snowdaymagazine

SNOWDAYMAGAZINE.COM

I'VE GOT YOUR BACK.

Treating a Class as a Family Unit Fosters Comfort, Consistency, and a Feeling of Home

by Author and 2nd Grade Teacher Shannon Olsen

I know you didn't go into teaching for the salary, but you deserve a raise!

Most people don't realize all of the work that it takes to build a strong, positive classroom community. It's not as though it's magically there when the kids show up in the seats that first week of school, and it's not because some teacher just got "lucky" with the group of students she was given. If a class has a wonderful sense of community, it's because the teacher worked very hard to make it that way.

It's so important to prioritize class community because it's the determining factor for everything else that happens in a classroom. It has a direct effect on academic success, student behavior, and even the teacher's mental health. Teachers teach best and kids learn best in an environment where individuals feel safe, loved, and accepted.

Something I often tell my student teachers is that while it's extremely important to get to know the kids and build personal connections with them, it's even more important for students to respect you than to like you (especially in the beginning).

Of course we want the kids to like us, but a truly ideal teacher-student relationship can't consist of just warm and fuzzy connections alone. If it did, our job title would be "friend" instead of "teacher." Just like kids need it from their parents, they also need structure and clearly set guidelines.

And the funny thing is, the kids will actually like you even more (even during those times when you might have to be a little hard on them) when there are those clear expectations.

They find comfort in consistency and fairness. So when I think of an ideal teacher-student relationship, it's an interpersonal one that is built on the foundation of respect.

"Something I hope to instill in my daughters as they start to get older is that if something is truly important to you, you will find a way to make time instead of excuses."

FAMILY MINDSET

I think teaching classroom community is something that starts from the very first day of school, or even prior. You can set the tone before school even begins by reaching out to students and their families. This can be done via email, a handwritten postcard, a welcome phone call, etc. Reaching out before the school year starts isn't necessary of course, but I think it does make for a positive first impression in sending the message that you're a teacher who genuinely cares and puts in extra effort for your kids.

The first day and first few weeks of school are essential for laying the foundation for class community. It's the time for all the get-to-know-you and team building activities that encourage students to make connections with each other. It's very worthwhile to focus on growth mindset and social emotional learning as well.

After a few weeks of dedicating time to these lessons and activities, I have the class collaborate in writing a Class Mission Statement. I pose the question, "What do we want for our classroom family this year?" I ask them what things they think we need to do on a daily basis so that they can learn as best they can and be happy at school.

I have them brainstorm, and I write their ideas onto a circle map. After that, we prioritize the ones they think are most important. We work together in stretching those ideas into sentences, and then putting them in order in a way that makes sense to create our official Class Mission Statement (this is done in a Word Document on the computer, which I project up onto a screen so that we can create and edit together).

Once the Mission Statement is complete, I have some of the kids write the finished product onto sentence strips and I display them on a poster. Each student signs their name around it to show that they are in agreement. We read it every day during Morning Meeting (the kids come up with hand motions to go with it). It's a positive way to start each day and get them into a good mindset.

I wrote *Our Class is a Family* because it's the type of book I wanted to read aloud to my own class. I was wishing that there was a read aloud (especially for the first day of school) that expressed the idea that our class is just like a family, and it didn't exist. So I just decided to go for it and create one! I had dreamed of being an author one day since I was a kid in school myself, and this seemed like the perfect opportunity, especially since it was a way to help serve fellow educators at the same time.

The primary aim of the book is to help kids and teachers, plain and simple. The hope is that it will help teachers strengthen the bond they have with their students, and that their students have with each other. My other major hope for the book is that it might help more kids feel a sense of belonging at school, especially during this unprecedented time they've been going through with distance learning.

When a teacher reads this book aloud to their students, they are sending the message that their class

is a special kind of family. Families care about each other, support one another, and have fun together! They also make mistakes together and help each other grow. Teachers and students spend more time together on average than their actual families, so we might as well make our classrooms feel like a home away from home.

Just like most teachers, I want students to treat each other the way that they want to be treated, with respect and kindness.

I do not believe this is something that can be taught once, and then all the kids have "got it." It has to be taught continually throughout the year. It takes a solid mix of reading aloud books about kindness, direct lessons and activities about being respectful to others, and real life learning opportunities. It's those little heart-to-heart chats you have with a couple kids after a squabble on the playground. It's praising students when you catch them doing a random act of kindness.

And it's also about setting an example for our kids. Even when we think they're not paying attention, students notice the way we interact with other teachers when we pass by them walking in line, the way we speak with the custodian or the school secretary over the phone, etc. We have to model the way that we should treat others.

TEACHER HACK

My favorite organization hack is to hole punch sticky notes and put them over hangers to use as "dividers" for my chart rack. This helps me find what charts I need more quickly.

For many of my charts, I make the title and the border and then laminate so that I can reuse them again. I just write on it with white board marker and erase, or have the kids write responses on Post-Its to stick on there. It saves a lot of chart paper, as well as a lot of time in making nicer letters for the headings, etc.

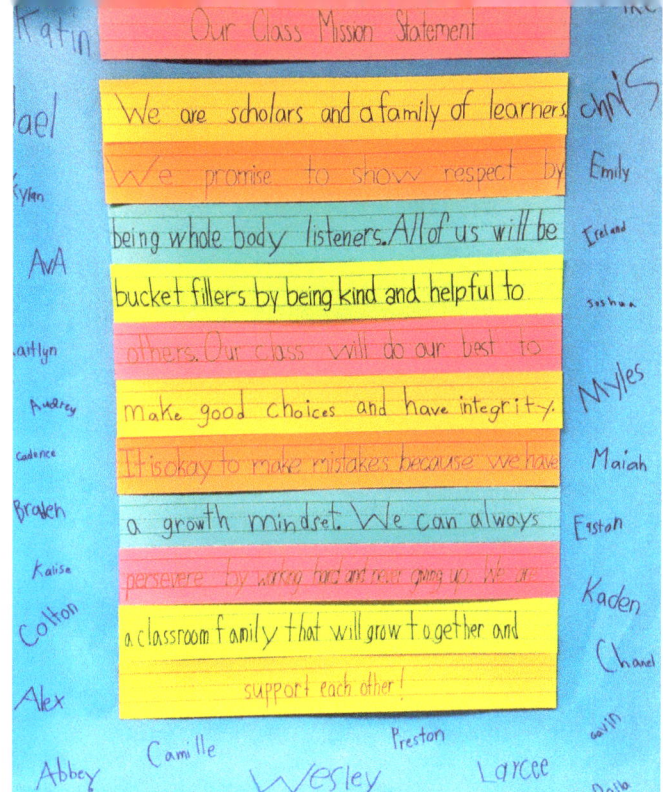

I work at a school that does not have a traditional calendar year, or a standard summer vacation. The school is divided into 4 tracks: A, B, C, and D. Only 3 tracks are in session at any given time, and the 4th is "off track," meaning that they are on break. So it's like one big revolving door where 25% of the school takes turns each month going on break. I teach for 3 months, then I have a month off. And repeat.

The reason for the year round schedule is that the area I teach in is densely populated. It allows for more students to be able to be enrolled in the school. This has its pros and cons. Here are some of the main ones (this is my own opinion, of course):

PROS:
- Teacher burnout is not as severe. We get to "recharge our batteries" every 3 months with a break.

- It's ideal for people like me, who love to travel. I can plan trips with my family during off peak times, meaning less crowds and better deals on airfare and hotels.

CONS:
- It can make planning with the entire grade level a challenge. Many of us are at different points in the curriculum at any given time.

- The biggest negative, right here: We have to rotate classrooms three times a year. Every time I go off track, I have to pack up my entire classroom so that the next track can come into the room. When I return, I have to set it up all over again in a new room. Since you are probably a teacher and know how much work goes into setting up and taking down a classroom, your mind is probably spinning just thinking about it.

The great news? A brand new school is opening in our district this year, and so our enrollment is now lower. This is the first time in 15 years that I will not have to rotate classrooms! Happy dance!

The basics:
I'm from Southern California and have my teaching credential and Masters from University of California Irvine. I met my husband the same year I started my student teaching (not through teaching, it was somewhere super romantic instead…a bar, haha)! We're celebrating our 10th wedding anniversary this year. We have two young daughters who put a huge smile on my face daily, ages 4 and 6. I'm going into my 15th year of teaching second grade, and going into my 4th year of creating resources for teachers on TpT.

Interesting tidbit:
Whenever asked to "share one interesting fact about yourself" for a PD or icebreaker activity, one of the things I'll sometimes say is that I won the Showcase Showdown on the gameshow "The Price is Right!" I was a resident advisor in college for the freshmen dorms, and I took my residents on the game show as a bonding activity. To my complete surprise, I was called on as a contestant and ended up winning a ton of crazy prizes, including a piano and a Dodge Ram truck. And I also can't forget the vacuum cleaner with music headphones attached (I thoroughly enjoyed vacuuming and dancing around my apartment like Mrs. Doubtfire).

Q&A WITH SHANNON OLSEN

WHAT FUELS YOUR SOUL?

Aside from the obvious answers (my daughters, my husband, teaching, creating things for the classroom,) I would say travel. I live in a small place and I don't have a closet full of fancy shoes, but my passport is full! I've been to about 40 countries on 6 different continents. Ever since I studied abroad in Italy in college, I made a little promise to myself that I would try to travel to a new country at least once a year. And I'm grateful to say that I've actually stuck to that promise for almost twenty years now.

TELL US ABOUT YOUR OWN MENTOR / TEACHER

I did my first student teaching assignment in a third grade classroom. My supervising teacher was Patty Poveda, and I learned so much about classroom management and student engagement just from observing her. I still use a lot of her strategies in my own classroom years later.

HOW DO YOU GET INSPIRED FOR THE NEXT BIG THING?

I find inspiration everywhere (sometimes in the most random, weird places, like a gift shop at the airport), but mostly in the classroom. Most of the resources in my TpT store (and my book) came from ideas that I wanted or needed for my own students.

"My house is clean enough to be healthy, and messy enough to be happy."

WHAT DO YOU DO TO ENSURE YOUR WORKSPACE AND HOME SPACE ARE NURTURING?

I'm going to keep it real with you. I do not have a Pinterest-worthy workspace. I would love to have my own office when we eventually move to a bigger place, but my office is currently my couch!

As for my home space, I posted this quote on my Instagram page a while back, and it still holds true (especially during these past few months of quarantine) - "My house is clean enough to be healthy, and messy enough to be happy."

My home is not always in tip-top shape were there to be a surprise visit from in-laws, but it's a happy home. Many moms might agree that cleaning with little kids around can often feel like shoveling snow while snow is falling, and I've accepted that some days it's just a losing battle. I'll take quality time with my family and keeping up with work projects that are important to me over making sure that the floor is spotlessly free and clear of toys at all times.

Order Shannon's book, *Our Class is a Family*, on Amazon or get signed copies or discounts for bulk orders on the website.

Website: life-between-summers.com
Instagram: @lifebetweensummers
TpT: Life Between Summers

Dear Parents,

Have you heard about the widespread impact of sleep? It turns out that there have been links between sleep deficiency and things like ADHD, obesity, and depression in children and adolescents. Also, a good night's sleep is linked to enhanced physical and mental health. Here are some ways you can promote good "sleep hygiene" in your child:

Misdiagnosed ADHD, Depression, and other Issues Can Often Actually be Attributed to Lack of Sleep

IN THE U.S. 38% OF KIDS AND 73% OF HIGH SCHOOL TEENS DO NOT GET ENOUGH SLEEP

>> Enforce a strict bedtime (Your child should be getting at least _____ hours of sleep per night.) Remove electronics an hour before bedtime. Keep all cell phones and other devices in a living space, or even in a parent's bedroom overnight. **Parents tend to underestimate the amount of time their child spends online in the bedroom.**

>> Establish a consistent bedtime routine (include things like brushing teeth, bathing, and reading). For older students, spend a few minutes talking each evening before bed. They may be able to clear their minds by getting important things out and off their chests before resting. Some students benefit from having a white noise machine or nature sounds.

>> Have your child wake up around the same time each morning.

>> Make sure their room is quiet and dark all through the night.

>> Stay positive! If your child isn't sleeping well, keep trying. If problems persist, talk to your doctor.

Here are some guidelines on the recommended hours of sleep:
Infants under 1 year: 12-16 hours
Children 1-2 years old: 11-14 hours
Children 3-5 years old: 10-13 hours
Children 6-12 years old: 9-12 hours
Teenagers 13-18 years old: 8-10 hours

OUR CHILDREN AND TEENS ARE SLEEP DEPRIVED, AND WE'RE MISSING THE SIGNALS, OR WORSE, MISDIAGNOSING WHAT'S GOING ON.

Inspiration from... FLANNERY O'CONNOR

The truth does not change according to our ability to stomach it.

Conviction without experience makes for harshness.

Faith is what someone knows to be true, whether they believe it or not.

The basis of art is truth, both in matter and in mode.

It is better to be young in failures than old in successes.

I find that most people know what a story is until they sit down to write one.

I do not know you, God, because I am in the way. Please help me to push myself aside.

www.ingramcontent.com/pod-product-compliance
Lightning Source LLC
Chambersburg PA
CBHW042038100526
44587CB00030B/4478